POSTCONVICTION RELIEF

for the

FLORIDA PRISONER

Loren Rhoton

Postconviction Relief for the Florida Prisoner
A publication of Loren Rhoton, P.A.
©2013 Loren Rhoton

ISBN: 978-0-9822800-7-2

Loren Rhoton has dedicated his career to helping Florida inmates seek justice. In addition to providing criminal appeals and postconviction representation to individuals, Mr. Rhoton also volunteered his time and advice to the Florida Prison Legal Aid Organization (FPLAO). Mr. Rhoton sat on the Board of Directors of FPLAO and wrote a legal self-help column, Postconviction Corner, for FPLAO's publication, the Florida Prison Legal Perspectives. When FPLAO dissolved, Mr. Rhoton continued to offer his self-help articles in his own newsletter, the Florida Postconviction Journal. This book is a compilation of Mr. Rhoton's articles from FPLP and the Florida Postconviction Journal.

Contact Loren Rhoton, P.A., at:
412 E. Madison Street
Suite 1111
Tampa, Florida 33602
lorenrhoton@rhotonpostconviction.com
rhotonpostconviction.com

CONTENTS

INTRODUCTION to POSTCONVICTION RELIEF

You are currently incarcerated and do not feel that you have been treated fairly by the judicial system for one reason or another. You went to trial and do not feel that you were adequately represented by your attorney. You feel that your sentence is illegal and excessive. Although you have already seen your direct appeal through to its conclusion, you may still have the ability to attack your sentence.

This article will address the possibilities and pitfalls that accompany postconviction collateral attacks on criminal judgments and sentences. Whether you intend to represent yourself (*pro se*) in your quest for postconviction relief or whether you will retain an attorney, you should go into such a venture fully informed. Although it would be impossible to apprise a potential postconviction litigant of every possibility, the aim of this and future articles is to help the convicted person understand the confusing and difficult field that is postconviction law.

There is nothing more frustrating for me than when a potential client has me investigate his or her case and I have to tell that client: "You had a great case three years ago, but there is nothing that we can do about it now." I have had this scenario arise countless times in my career. I have seen many people who, after pursuing their direct appeal, gave up on the possibility of any relief from the sentence they are serving. Some people do not pursue relief because they are depressed about their situation and feel it is futile to waste their time, effort, and money when all they have seen are negative results up to that point. Other people fail to timely assert their rights because of misinformation they have received from people not trained, or inadequately trained, in the law. And still others do not proceed with a postconviction case because they cannot afford legal representation and are afraid to step into the legal area *pro se* (not represented by counsel).

Whatever the reason, if you do not actively seek postconviction relief while you can, you will likely regret it later. For the people that can afford legal counsel, I recommend that you do so immediately. For those who are indigent and cannot find *pro bono* representation, I recommend that you educate yourself on the law and seek advice from law clerks at your institution. If you hesitate, you may be waiving important legal rights.

In Florida there are several Rules of Criminal Procedure that provide for a postconviction attack on a criminal conviction and/or sentence. Florida Rule of Criminal Procedure 3.800 provides that an illegal sentence (one that exceeds the maximums by law) can be attacked at any time. Therefore, if your sentence is illegal there is no time limit for filing a motion to correct such a sentence. However, if your wish to raise other issues, such as the denial of effective assistance of counsel or other deprivations of constitutional rights, you will need to file a Florida Rule of Criminal Procedure 3.850 Motion for Postconviction Relief (3.850).

A 3.850 motion does have a two-year period of limitations that begins running from the date that your judgment and sentence is final. Your sentence is, generally, final at one of two times:

(1) if you did not appeal your Judgment and Sentence the sentence is final at the time it is imposed by the trial court; or

(2) if you did appeal your Judgment and Sentence the sentence is final at the time that the appellate court's mandate is issued.

The two-year period of limitations begins running at the later of the two dates. The two year period limitation is a fairly strict requirement and there are only a few exceptions to filing a 3.850 motion outside of the two years.

Furthermore, for the purpose of preserving the right to later attack your conviction in the federal courts (if necessary) a 3.850 motion should be filed within one year of when the sentence is final.

Therefore, the first and most important advice that I can give is ***do not hesitate***. If you let the two-year period of limitations lapse without filing your 3.850, the chances are slim that you will obtain postconviction relief.

It is also important to seek licensed legal counsel if at all possible. Often inmates rely upon law clerks to help them pursue relief. If you are unable to afford counsel, then I recommend that you do seek out the help of such clerks. It is true that there are some excellent law clerks within the institutions. However, there is an immense benefit of having experienced, licensed, postconviction counsel who can more freely deal with the courts on your behalf. The unfortunate reality is that *pro se* motions are not, in my opinion, taken as seriously by the courts. Furthermore, I have often seen that persons who pursue their postconviction actions *pro se* may have a good understanding of the legal issues but still might not understand the procedural aspects of their case. Therefore, an improperly filed or inartfully drafted postconviction motion may end up barring well-deserved relief.

Ineffective assistance of counsel ("IAC") claims are probably the most common grounds raised in postconviction motions. However, courts are generally reluctant to find ineffectiveness of counsel in criminal proceedings. It has been estimated that the national success rate for IAC claims is approximately 3.9%. The odds are already not in your favor on IAC claims. Without experienced counsel in your corner it is just one more strike against you.

If you do decide to retain counsel, make sure he is experienced in appellate and postconviction matters. Although an attorney may be a great trial attorney, that does not mean that he has an understanding of postconviction matters. Postconviction matters are often hybrid types of cases that require experience in courtroom matters and the ability to craft well-written, appellate-type arguments on the client's behalf. Often, trial attorneys are not experienced with appellate matters and prefer not to get involved with the extensive legal research and writing that is required in a postconviction case.

If you are looking for an attorney, ask around to see what the attorney's reputation is. The best way to learn if an attorney is good is to ask people he or she has represented. Also, do not be afraid to ask an attorney questions before you hire him. If you are going to be paying good money, you want to make sure that you are not throwing it away. Ask your attorney for his written qualifications. These will be a good indication as to whether or not the attorney is experienced in the postconviction field.

There are also a number of things you should be on the lookout for when looking for a good attorney to help you with your case. First and foremost: ***do not retain an attorney that promises you a certain result in your case***. Any person that guarantees you a result on your case is lying to you. No attorney, no matter how good, can look into the future and tell you what a court will do. It is highly unethical and outright dishonest for an attorney to guarantee results. Such a promise by an attorney is indicative of a lack of ethics and is likely a precursor to shoddy legal work. You are better off with an attorney that is honest with you and tells you his or her opinion on your case without a guarantee of results.

An attorney's experience in postconviction matter is of the utmost importance if you intend to try to collaterally attack your judgment and sentence. Thus, it is important to ask the attorney how many cases like yours he has handled. You may also want to find out if the attorney has handled any cases where he has garnered written opinions from appellate courts; this will be a good indicator of the attorney's experience with postconviction matters. And, while an attorney's previous successes in postconviction cases may be impressive, always be aware that each case is different. It is good to know that your attorney is experienced, but, do not take an attorney's prior successes as a promise of positive results in your case.

In closing, it is vitally important that you not hesitate if you intend to collaterally attack your judgment and sentence. Do not waive your legal rights to attack your conviction. If you can manage to retain counsel, do so; if not, educate yourself immediately on your case and how you can attack it. In future articles I will delve into specific matters relating to postconviction issues and give hints and tips for both those who are represented by counsel and those who are representing themselves in their quest for relief.

RULE 3.850
and COGNIZABLE CLAIMS

In my last article I tried to give a general outline of the different types of State postconviction remedies available to convicted persons. In this article I will address one of the most important postconviction attacks. After the direct appeal, the most common vehicle for attacking a Judgment and Sentence is the Florida Rule of Criminal 3.850 Motion for Postconviction Relief, commonly referred to as a "three-point-eight-five-oh" or a "thirty-eight-fifty".

People untrained in postconviction matters often inform me that someone has advised them to file a petition for writ of habeas corpus to address certain deprivations of constitutional rights in their case. These people are usually misinformed as Rule 3.850 is essentially a codification of the right to file a habeas corpus petition. Rule 3.850(a) provides, in part, that a person convicted and sentenced of a crime can attack his or her judgment and sentence on the grounds that:

(1)   The judgment was entered or sentence was imposed in violation of the Constitution or laws of the United States or the State of Florida;

(2)   The court did not have jurisdiction to enter the judgment;

(3)   The court did not have jurisdiction to impose the sentence;

(4)   The sentence exceeded the maximum authorized by law;

(5)   The plea was involuntary; or,

(6)   The judgment or sentence is otherwise subject to collateral
        attack.

Rule 3.850 offers many possibilities for attacking a conviction and sentence. However, there are also a good number of issues that one cannot raise in a 3.850 motion. I have often seen petitioners try to raise issues in their 3.850 motions which, if at all, should have been raised on their direct appeals. This is improper and will not obtain relief. Issues that were, or should have been, raised on direct appeal are not cognizable in a 3.850 motion. See, *Jackson v. State*, 646 So.2d 792 (Fla. 2nd DCA 1994). Typically issues which were, or should have been, raised on direct appeal tend to deal with improper rulings of law by the trial courts.

It is important to take note of the issues that are not addressable in a 3.850 motion and avoid presenting them in your postconviction motion. I have seen far too many *pro se* motions which contain twenty or more issues, when only two or three of the issues have merit. The approach of "shotgunning" your motion and including any and every imaginable claim does nothing but harm your chance for relief. The more you include bad issues in your motion, the more you lose credibility in relation to your meritorious issues. Therefore, for the *pro se* postconviction movant, I strongly recommend presenting a well-crafted 3.850 motion presenting only the issues that really have a chance of obtaining relief. If you hand a court a forty page motion containing fifteen issues, your motion is automatically going to be suspect to the court and you will lose much needed credibility.

Rivera v. Dugger, 629 So.2d 105 (Fla. 1993) gives a number of good examples of issues that are proper for direct appeal, and thus improper for a 3.850, including:

- ◆   whether the defendant was prejudiced by his absence from
        certain proceedings.
- ◆   whether alleged failures of a translator prejudiced the
        defendant.
- ◆   whether the jury instructions were adequate.

- the denial of the defendant's right to cross-examine witnesses.
- whether the trial court improperly dismissed a juror for cause.
- whether the presence of uniformed police at the trial prejudiced the defendant.

Other issues which are proper for direct appeal, instead of a 3.850, include but are not limited to: competency to stand trial [*Johnson v. Dugger*, 583 So.2d 657 (Fla. 1991)]; speedy trial claims [*Waldburg v. State*, 644 So.2d 608 (Fla. 1st DCA 1994)]; improper arguments or misconduct of the prosecutor [*Blanco v. Wainwright*, 507 So.2d 1377 (Fla. 1987)]; jury selection issues [*Lambrix v. State*, 559 So.2d 1137 (Fla. 1990)]; sufficiency of the evidence [*Williams v. State*, 642 So.2d 67 (Fla. 1st DCA 1994)]; admissibility of evidence [*Engle v. Dugger*, 576 So.2d 696 (Fla. 1991)]; and, defects in the charging documents [*Williams v. State*, 642 So.2d 67 (Fla. 1st DCA 1994)].

While the above issues are proper for the direct appeal, circuit courts often have difficulty differentiating between them and ineffectiveness of counsel claims relating to the above issues. For example, a 3.850 might raise a claim of ineffectiveness of counsel for trial counsel's failure to object to improper prosecutorial arguments. It would not be uncommon for a circuit court to deny relief on the claim and assert that it was a claim that should have been raised on direct appeal. In denying such claims, circuit court's will often use language such as *Rule 3.850 is not a vehicle for obtaining a second appeal of issues which were raised or should have been raised on appeal* or *allegations of ineffective assistance of counsel will not be permitted to serve as a means of circumventing the rule that 3.850 proceedings do not provide a second or substitute appeal.* Such attempts on the part of a court are outright improper. It is often appropriate to point out to a court (in a motion for rehearing) that the claim being asserted is one of ineffectiveness of counsel and that the general rule is that ineffectiveness of counsel claims are generally not cognizable on appeal when the issue has not been raised in trial court. *See, Blanco v. Wainwright*, 507 So.2d 1377 (Fla. 1987). Just keep in mind that a motion for rehearing must be filed with the circuit court within fifteen (15) days of the order denying a 3.850. F.R.Cr. P. 3.850(g).

Before getting into the issues that can be presented in your 3.850 there are some procedural rules that must be taken into consideration. Firstly, pursuant to Florida Rule of Criminal Procedure 3.850(b) you must (in most circumstances) file your 3.850 within two years of the time that your sentence becomes final. The two-year time limitation for filing motions for postconviction relief pursuant to Rule 3.850 does not begin to run until appellate proceedings have concluded and the court issues a mandate or thirty days after the judgment and sentence become final if no direct appeal is filed. *See, Gust v. State,* 535 So.2d 642 (Fla. 1st DCA 1988); and, *Saavedra v. State,* 59 So.3d 191, 192 (Fla. 3rd DCA2011). The two-year period of limitations is a fairly strict requirement and there are only a few exceptions to filing a 3.850 motion outside of the two years. Furthermore, for the purpose of preserving your right to later attack your conviction in the federal courts, a 3.850 should be filed within one year of when the sentence is final.

Additionally, it is important to plan ahead and, if possible, present all meritorious postconviction issues in one 3.850 motion. If you try to present your issues to the court in a piecemeal fashion (i.e., filing numerous 3.850 motions containing different issues) you will possibly be denied relief on your later motions because said motions will be considered successive or an abuse of procedure. Florida Rule of Criminal Procedure 3.850(f) provides that "[a] second or successive motion may be dismissed if the judge finds that it fails to allege new or different grounds for relief and the prior determination was on the merits". Or, your motion can be dismissed when you raise new and different grounds "if the judge finds that the failure of the movant or the attorney to assert those grounds in a prior motion constituted an abuse of procedure . . . ". FRCrP 3.850(f). To put it simply: present all of your meritorious grounds in one well-prepared motion or you may risk having them later dismissed.

Also a 3.850 is limited to 50 pages. FRCrP 3.850(c). A 3.850 that exceeds the page limit without leave of the court will likely be dismissed. This is another reason that it is good practice to weed out weak issues and present only the strong claims.

The grounds that can be raised in a 3.850 motion include, but are not limited to:

- The movant's plea was induced by threats or promises. *Thompson v. State*, 570 So.2d 1098 (Fla. 2nd DCA 1990).

- Double Jeopardy Claims. *Ferenc v. State*, 563 So.2d 707 (Fla. 1st DCA 1990).

- Use of Perjured Testimony *Conyers v. State*, 215 So.2d 616 (Fla .3rd DCA 1968).

- Recantation of testimony by key witnesses. *Norris v. State*, 586 So. 2d 1320 (Fla. 2d DCA 1991); *Roberts v. State*, 678 So. 2d 1332 (Fla. 1996).

- Newly discovered evidence. See, *Melendez v. State*, 718 So.2d 746 (Fla. 1998).

One of the most used issues in 3.850s is the allegation that a criminal defendant was deprived of his 6th Amendment Right to effective assistance of counsel. The 6th Amendment provides that in all criminal prosecutions " . . . the accused shall . . . have the assistance of Counsel for his defense." The U.S. Supreme Court has interpreted the right to counsel to mean the right to effective counsel. In order to demonstrate ineffective assistance of counsel, a defendant must prove both that his counsel performed deficiently and that the performance actually prejudiced the defendant. *Strickland v. Washington*, 466 U.S. 668 (1984). The two prongs of the ineffectiveness inquiry are independent of one another, and thus, must both be proved to establish a claim of ineffective assistance of counsel. *Id.* at 697. In order to satisfy the "performance" prong of the *Strickland* test a defendant must show that his counsel's representation fell below an objective standard of reasonableness. *Id.* at 687-688. In *Lockhart v. Fretwell*, 506 U.S. 364 (1993), The Supreme Court explained that "the 'prejudice' component of the *Strickland* test . . . focuses on the question whether counsel's deficient performance renders the result of the trial unreliable or the proceedings fundamentally unfair."

"Ineffective Assistance of Counsel" (IAC) claims are numerous and wide ranging. One of the more commonly raised IAC grounds is that defense counsel was ineffective for failing to investigate some aspect of the client's case. An attorney can be ineffective for failing to investigate favorable witnesses. An attorney has the duty to interview and examine as many as possible of the persons who are supposed to know the facts so as to be able to ascertain the truth concerning the charge in controversy and to prepare a defense thereto. *Mathews v. State*, 44 So.2d 664 (Fla. 1950). An attorney's failure to interview and call such witnesses and to conduct an adequate pretrial investigation by seeking out potential witnesses can constitute ineffective assistance of counsel. *Sorgman v. State*, 549 So.2d 686 (Fla. 1st DCA 1989).

Additionally, an attorney has the duty to investigate and possibly present any potential defenses for his or her client. The failure of an attorney to pursue a legitimate defense on behalf of a client in a criminal proceeding can constitute ineffective assistance of counsel. See, *Foster v. Lockhart*, 9 F.3d 722 (8th Cir. 1993) [failure of attorney to argue impotency defense to rape charge was ineffective assistance of counsel]; and, *Profitt v. Waldron*, 831 F.2d 1245 (5th Cir. 1987) [failure to raise insanity defense was ineffective assistance of counsel where attorney knew defendant had escaped a mental institution prior to committing a crime].

A prime example of an attorney's failure to investigate a defense is demonstrated in *Bridges v. State*, 466 So.2d 348 (4th DCA 1985). In *Bridges* the defendant was convicted of two counts of aggravated assault. The defendant filed a Rule 3.850 motion alleging that his attorney was ineffective because he failed to pursue a defense of voluntary intoxication. *Id.* at 348. Trial counsel did not raise the involuntary intoxication defense because he did not feel that the defendant's intoxication met the statutory requirements for a jury instruction. *Id.* at 348. However, in *Bridges* there was evidence that the defendant had been drinking for several hours prior to the offenses. *Id.* at 348. Additionally witnesses described the defendant as being "berserk", "unstable", "half-there", and "a whole lot strung out," prior to the commission of the offense. *Id.* The *Bridges* Court held that trial counsel's failure to present the involuntary intoxication defense was ineffective and reversed and remanded the case for a new trial. *Id.* at 348-349. In support of its decision the court stated that "in light of [the evidence available to counsel], competent counsel would have pursued an intoxication defense. *Id.* at 348.

Additional Ineffective Assistance of Counsel Claims include, but are not limited to:

- Misadvice as to how much time the defendant will actually have to serve. *Garmon v Lockhart*, 938 F.2d 120 (8th Cir. 1991): *Ricardo v. State*, 647 So.2d 287 (Fla. 2nd DCA 1994).
- Failure to present mitigation evidence in the penalty phase of a trial. *Hildwin v. Dugger*, 654 So.2d 107 (Fla. 1995).
- Failure to suppress illegally obtained evidence. *Kimmelman v. Morrison*, 477 U.S. 365 (1986).
- Failure to impeach adverse witnesses. *Smith v. Wainwright*, 741 F.2d 1248 (11th Cir. 1984).
- Failure of counsel to disclose a conflict of interest to his or her client. *Cuyler v. Sullivan*, 446 U.S. 335 (1980).
- Failure to object to prosecutorial misconduct. *United States v. Wolf*, 784 F.2d 1094 (7th Cir. 1986); and, *Gordon v. State*, 469 So.2d 795 (4th DCA 1985).
- Failure to move to withdraw a client's plea of *nolo contendere*. *Holtan v. Parrat*, 683 F.2d 1163 (8th Cir.1982).

The above cited ineffectiveness of counsel cases are but a small example of claims regarding the deficiencies of counsel. There are many more issues that can be raised in regards to ineffectiveness of counsel. In fact, it is often possible to allege in a 3.850 that all of trial counsel's deficiencies, when taken together, served to deprive the movant of his or her right to a fair trial. Therefore, the cumulative impact of a defense attorney's deficiencies at trial can prejudice a defendant and thus deprive him of his 6th Amendment right to effective assistance of counsel. *Harris by and through Ramseyer v. Wood*, 64 F.3d 1432 (9th Cir. 1995); See also *Mak v. Blodgett*, 970 F.2d 614 (9th Cir. 1992) [" . . . significant errors occurred that, considered cumulatively, compel affirmance of the district court's grant of habeas corpus as to the sentence of death."]; See also *Cooper v. Fitzsimmons*, 586 F.2d 1325 (9th Cir. 1972) ["prejudice may result from cumulative impact of multiple deficiencies."]. This is so even where no single error of omission of the counsel, standing alone, significantly impairs the defense. *Ewing v. Williams*, 596 F.2d 391 (9th Cir. 1979).

It is apparent that there are a wide variety of ineffectiveness of counsel claims that may be available to one in a 3.850 motion. A thorough review of the above cited cases will hopefully point the *pro se* movant in the right direction in preparing a 3.850 based on ineffectiveness of counsel. It is important to keep in mind that in making any ineffectiveness claim, one always must be aware of the *Strickland* standard and be able to demonstrate how the claims satisfy the *Strickland* test. Merely demonstrating one of the prongs of the test will not obtain relief. If you can clearly demonstrate both prongs of *Strickland* to your trial court, your chances of obtaining postconviction relief will definitely increase.

3.850 PREPARATION
and SUMMARY DENIAL

In my last article I explained the purpose of Florida Rule of Criminal Procedure 3.850 (hereinafter "3.850") and tried to give a number of good examples of what types of claims can be brought under Rule 3.850. This article will further address Rule 3.850 and how to proceed once your 3.850 Motion has been filed. Of course the goal of filing a 3.850 motion is to overturn your conviction and/or sentence. In attempting to overturn a conviction, the postconviction movant must be aware that there are numerous hurdles which must be cleared before relief can or will be granted. The first such hurdle is to obtain an evidentiary hearing at which the trial court will consider the issues presented in your 3.850.

As the trial courts are generally reluctant to seriously consider postconviction claims, it is not unusual for a trial court to summarily deny a 3.850 motion without granting an evidentiary hearing. A 3.850 can be summarily denied for any number of reasons. Thus, it is good to be aware of such factors and try to avoid the summary dismissal of your motion. Firstly, it important that the facts presented in your 3.850 motion be sworn to under the penalties of perjury. Florida Rule of Criminal Procedure 3.987 provides a Model Motion for Postconviction Relief that will prove helpful to the *pro se* postconviction litigant who is preparing his or her own motion. At the end of the Model Motion there are two sample oaths, a notarized oath and an un-notarized oath. It is imperative that you include one of said oaths (it does not matter which) at the end of your 3.850. Otherwise your motion will be summarily dismissed as not complying with the Rules of Criminal Procedure. Additionally, if a supporting memorandum is filed along with the 3.850, said memorandum must also be sworn to under oath. *Brown v. State*, 620 So.2d 1076 (Fla. 2nd DCA 1993).

Additionally, a 3.850 must sufficiently allege the facts that support any claims being made in the motion. Alleging only conclusions of law in your 3.850 will not be sufficient to get an evidentiary hearing and will likely be grounds for a summary dismissal. For example, the bare legal conclusion that an attorney was ineffective for failing to investigate a voluntary intoxication defense will be insufficient to obtain an evidentiary hearing. But, assertions that the defendant was intoxicated when his offenses occurred and that he told counsel of his intoxication are sufficient allegations to garner an evidentiary hearing. *Harley v. State*, 753 So.2d 693 (4th DCA 2000). Thus it is crucial that sufficient facts be alleged to support any legal conclusions made in your motion.

Also, it is important to be aware of the page limitations imposed by Rule 3.850. A 3.850 motion and any supporting memorandum is limited to 50 pages. Fla.R.Crim.P. 3.850(c). A 3.850 that exceeds the page limit will likely be dismissed unless the court has already granted leave to exceed the limit. The page limit only applies to substantive matters and does not include additional pages attached as exhibits to the motion. *Adams v. State*, 104 So.3d 1141 (Fla. 2nd DCA, 2012).

Another reason that a 3.850 can be summarily dismissed is if the motion was not filed within the two-year time limit that is imposed pursuant to Florida Rule of Criminal Procedure 3.850(b). A presumption exists that an inmate's legal document is timely filed if: (1) it contains a certificate of service showing that the pleading was placed in the hands of prison or jail officials for mailing on a particular date; and, (2) that the pleading would have been timely filed if it had been received and file-stamped by the court on that particular date. *Thompson v. State*, 761 So.2d 324 (Fla. 2000). There are only a few exceptions to the two-year period of limitations. Florida Rule of Criminal Procedure 3.850(b) provides three such exceptions:

(1)   *Newly Discovered Evidence*: the claims on which the motion is predicated must have been unknown to the movant or the movant's attorney and could not have been ascertained by the exercise of due diligence. The newly discovered evidence must be of such a nature that it would probably produce an acquittal on retrial. *Jones v. State*, 591 So.2d 911 (Fla.1991). Alternatively, if there was a plea, it must be shown that withdrawal of the plea is necessary to correct a manifest injustice. *Bradford v. State*, 869 So.2d 28 (Fla. 2nd DCA 2004); and, *Deck v. Jones*, 985 So.2nd 1234 (Fla. 2nd DCA 2008).

(2)   *New Case Law*: it must be demonstrated that a fundamental constitutional right was not established within the time frame of the movant's case and that such fundamental right has been held to apply retroactively. *See, State v. Callaway*, 658 So.2d 983 (Fla. 1995), for test to determine retroactivity of new case law.

(3)   If the movant retained an attorney to timely file a 3.850 motion and counsel, through neglect, failed to file the motion. *See, Steele v. Kehoe*, 747 So.2d 931(Fla. 1999).

Unless one of the above exceptions applies, an untimely 3.850 will be summarily dismissed by the trial court.

Even if a 3.850 motion satisfies all of the aforementioned procedural requirements, said motion can still be summarily denied by the trial court if the record conclusively demonstrates that the postconviction movant is not entitled to relief. Florida Rule of Criminal Procedure 3.850(d) provides in part that: "[i]f the motion, files, and records in the case conclusively show that the movant is entitled to no relief, the motion shall be denied without a hearing." Rule 3.850(d) further provides that if the court's summary denial of a 3.850 is not based on the legal insufficiency of the claims, a copy of those portions of the files and records that conclusively refute the claims must be attached to the order denying relief. *Hoffman v. State*, 571 So.2d 449 (Fla. 1990). The failure of the trial court to include the supporting attachments requires a reversal and remand of the trial court's order so that the trial court can either attach the proper supporting documents or hold an evidentiary hearing on the grounds asserted by the movant. *Jefferson v. State*, 638 So.2d 123 (Fla. 1st DCA 1994).

If a trial court does summarily deny a 3.850 and attaches documents to the order denying the motion, it is important to determine if the documents attached actually support the trial court's denial. Sometimes the documents that the court attaches to its order will actually support the claims asserted in the 3.850. In *Dames v. State*, 773 So.2d 563 (Fla. 2nd DCA 2000), the defendant filed a 3.850 alleging that his attorney was ineffective by failing to advise the defendant that his testimony would be necessary in order for the jury to be instructed on self-defense. The circuit court issued an order summarily denying the defendant's 3.850 and attached a portion of the trial transcripts to support such a denial. The portions of the transcripts showed that counsel argued for the self-defense instruction and that the trial court ruled against him. In *Dames*, the appellate court noted that the attached transcript in fact showed that the lower court denied the self-defense instruction solely because there was no evidence presented to support the self-defense instruction. As such, the *Dames* Court held that "[t]his tends to support, rather than refute [the defendant's claim] that his counsel should have had him testify to support the defense." *Id. Dames*, thus, demonstrates that just because a court attaches court files to a summary denial, it does not necessarily make the denial proper.

Another reason it is important to review the court's attachments to the summary denial is that such attachments may not actually qualify as part of the "files" and "records" that Rule 3.850 requires the court to attach to its order. Sometimes a court will try to attach documents which are outside of the court files to support a summary denial of a 3.850. This is improper and grounds for reversal. Consequently, the State's response to a 3.850 is not a record attachment as is contemplated by the Rules of Criminal Procedure and the Rules of Appellate Procedure, and, consequently, cannot be used as justification for the summary denial of a 3.850 motion. See, *Flores v. State*, 662 So.2d 1350 (Fla. 2nd DCA 1995).

Furthermore, documents prepared to refute claims in a postconviction motion are not to be used as substitutes for an evidentiary hearing. As a result, it is improper for the court to rely on affidavits in summarily denying a 3.850; affidavits generally cannot substitute for live testimony, subject to cross-examination, in proceedings under Florida Rule of Criminal Procedure 3.850. *Cintron v. State*, 508 So.2d 1315 (Fla. 2d DCA1987). In summarily denying a 3.850 it is also improper for a court to rely on a written statement by a defense attorney who is responding to allegations of ineffectiveness. *Bryant v. State*, 661 So.2d 73 (Fla. 2nd DCA 1995). Finally, if the court cites to pages of the trial transcripts in denying a 3.850, the court must attach copies of those transcript pages. See, *Flores v. State*, 662 So.2d 1350 (Fla. 2nd DCA 1995). Thus, if the trial court relies on any of the above types of documents in summarily denying a 3.850, said denial is improper and should be remanded for the lower court to either: (1) hold an evidentiary hearing; or, (2) attach those portions of the record which do support the summary denial.

If a court does summarily deny your 3.850, do not get discouraged. It is common for a trial court to dismiss a 3.850 without a hearing. The courts often do this in an attempt to make the case go away. However, this does not mean that you are out of luck. It just means that you will have to rely on the appellate process to get your issues remanded to the trial court. Often, if you can prevail on the appeal from a summary denial, the circuit court will just grant an evidentiary hearing instead of once again trying to attach record portions to a summary denial. Therefore, it is important to understand the procedural requirements of an appeal from the summary denial of a 3.850.

When a 3.850 is summarily denied, the postconviction litigant has several options. If the summary denial is going to be appealed, a notice of appeal must be filed with the circuit court within 30 days of the denial. *See* Florida Rule of Appellate Procedure 9.110(b). Florida Rule of Appellate Procedure 9.900(a) provides a form for the notice of appeal. [Note: in postconviction cases, it is not necessary to attach to the notice conformed copies of the order being appealed]. However, prior to filing the notice of appeal, it is important to first consider whether it might help to first file a motion for rehearing with the circuit court.

Rule 3.850(h) provides that a motion for rehearing may be filed with the circuit court within 15 days of the court's denial of the 3.850. It certainly does not hurt to file a motion for rehearing when a 3.850 is denied. In fact in some situations it may be the better way to get a circuit court to reconsider a 3.850. For example, if a 3.850 is filed without the proper sworn oath, the circuit court may summarily dismiss the 3.850. Such a dismissal is improper since under *Spera v. State*, 971 So.2d 754 (Fla. 2007) the trial court should have stricken the motion with leave to file an amended 3.850 with the proper oath attached. A summary dismissal such as the one mentioned above will likely be overturned on appeal in this circumstance, but the process can be shortened significantly by filing a motion for rehearing and avoiding an appeal.

In other situations it is up to the postconviction litigant to determine if he or she wishes to file for a rehearing or proceed directly to the appellate court. One important factor to consider is that the circuit court has already denied the motion once and will likely be reluctant to reverse itself. Another important consideration is that the appellate process is a time consuming one and filing for a rehearing may cause there to be additional delay in the final determination of the motion. Nevertheless, it does not hurt to file for a rehearing and on some occasions the circuit court may actually be willing to reverse itself.

If a motion for rehearing is filed after the summary denial of a 3.850, one should wait for the trial court's decision on the motion before filing a notice of appeal. If a notice of appeal is filed while the motion for rehearing is pending, the motion for rehearing will be deemed to have been waived and the trial court will be without jurisdiction to consider said motion. The filing of a notice of appeal vests the appellate court with complete and exclusive jurisdiction of the subject matter and parties to the appeal. *State ex rel. Faircloth v. The District Court of Appeal*, 187 So.2d 890 (Fla. 1966). Therefore, if a motion for rehearing is timely filed, it is best to be patient and wait for the trial court to decide the matter on rehearing before proceeding to the appellate court. Do not worry that you are waiving your rights to appeal by waiting to file the notice of appeal. If a timely motion for rehearing is filed, it will toll (extend) the 30 day time period for filing a notice of appeal. *See* Florida Rule of Appellate Procedure 9.020(j).

If the trial court denies your motion for rehearing or you have decided to forego such a motion, then it is time to move on to your appeal. When the trial court denies a 3.850 motion there is a 30 day window in which the case can be appealed. Florida Rule of Appellate Procedure 9.110(b) provides that a notice of appeal must be filed with the trial court within 30 days in order to invoke the jurisdiction of the appellate district court.

Typically when a notice of appeal is filed with the trial court, it is wise to file directions to the clerk of the circuit court informing the clerk what needs to be contained in the record on appeal. However, in the majority of the cases where a summary denial of a 3.850 is involved, the circuit court will not prepare a record on appeal. Instead the circuit court will forward copies of 3.850 motion and the court's order thereon to the appellate court. Therefore, if there are any other matters that you wish for the appellate court to consider on the appeal it is advisable to prepare and submit an appendix as is provided for in Rule of Appellate Procedure 9.220.

When you file your notice of appeal be aware that the time is then short to file a brief in support of any arguments you may have. No briefs or oral arguments are required in appeals from the summary judgment of a 3.850 motion. Nevertheless, it is advisable to submit an initial brief to the appellate court delineating the reasons that the summary denial of the 3.850 was improper. Pursuant to Rule of Appellate Procedure 9.141(b), if you intend to file an initial brief, such a brief must be filed within 15 days of the filing of the notice of appeal. Of course, for the *pro se* litigant it may be difficult to have such a brief prepared in the short period of time allowed. Therefore, if it will be impossible to have the brief timely filed, one may benefit from filing a motion for extension of time to file the initial brief. Although there is no guarantee that the appellate court will grant such a motion, the chances are good that it may buy a little bit of much needed time to make sure that a brief is submitted to the court before any decision is rendered.

In addressing the improper summary denial of a 3.850 on appeal it is always good to be aware of the lower court's obligation to attach record portions to its order denying relief. If such records are not attached to support the denial, the chances are good that the case will be remanded to the trial court. Additionally, as mentioned earlier, it is always good to review the attachments to the court's order to make sure that they actually do support the lower court's denial of your motion. Finally, one should be aware of some of the more typical ways that trial courts erroneously deny 3.850 motions.

Often, when there are claims of ineffective assistance of counsel, the trial courts will deny such claims and hold that the trial attorney's acts are justified by trial tactics. However, this is improper on the part of a trial court as such a conclusion is usually impossible to determine from the court files. A trial court's finding that some action or inaction by defense counsel was tactical is generally inappropriate without an evidentiary hearing. *Thomas v. State*, 634 So.2d 1157 (Fla. 1st DCA 1994). Therefore, a summary denial of an ineffectiveness of counsel claim based upon a finding of trial tactics will usually not support such a summary denial.

Additionally, it is common for a circuit court to deny relief on a claim of ineffective assistance of counsel by asserting that the claim should have been raised on direct appeal. In denying such claims circuit courts will often use language such as *Rule 3.850 is not a vehicle for obtaining a second appeal of issues which were raised or should have been raised on appeal* or *allegations of ineffective assistance of counsel will not be permitted to serve as a means of circumventing the rule that 3.850 proceedings do not provide a second or substitute appeal.* On appeal it is important to demonstrate that the claim asserted in the 3.850 was one of ineffectiveness of counsel and that the general rule is that ineffectiveness of counsel claims are generally not cognizable on a direct appeal when the issue has not been raised in the trial court. *See, Blanco v. Wainwright*, 507 So.2d 1377 (Fla. 1987)

Hopefully this article is helpful in understanding the way the trial courts try to deny 3.850 motions and the best ways to avoid a summary denial. Once again, if your 3.850 is summarily denied do not get discouraged. You still have the right to appeal such a denial and try to have your case remanded to the lower court for an evidentiary hearing. Your case is not over yet. Educate yourself in every way you can to determine the best way to pursue your case.

Once again, I hope that these articles are helpful in such an endeavor. The purpose of these articles is to inform inmates of the possible avenues of postconviction relief that may be available and how to pursue such avenues. In closing I would like to offer the following words of encouragement: Don't just lay down and let the courts run over you, instead, stand up and let them know that you are aware of your rights and that you know how to pursue them. Good luck with your postconviction pursuits until the next article.

3.850 EVIDENTIARY HEARINGS

In this article I will delve further into postconviction motions filed pursuant to Florida Rule of Criminal procedure 3.850. Up to this point I have addressed important issues that can be raised in a Rule 3.850 motion, the applicable rules and periods of limitation, and how to avoid having your 3.850 dismissed before the court has held an evidentiary hearing. As was previously explained, obtaining an evidentiary hearing is the first hurdle in an attempt to obtain postconviction relief. While getting an evidentiary hearing granted can be an accomplishment in and of itself in some courts, the challenging road to obtaining postconviction relief is still far from over at that point.

When an evidentiary hearing is granted on a 3.850, it is typical for a court to grant the hearing on some of the issues presented and summarily deny other issues in the motion. If this happens, do not despair that you have been denied relief on issues that you may have felt were strong. You will still have the opportunity to appeal the summary denial of those issues (if necessary) when the trial court has made its final decision after your evidentiary hearing. See *McCoy v. State*, 487 So.2d 1095 (Fla.1st DCA 1986)[an order is not final and appealable until it disposes of all the issues presented]. Therefore, the summarily denied issues cannot be raised on appeal until after all issues have been disposed of (and presumably denied if you are appealing the decision) through evidentiary hearing and/or summary denial.

If a court does grant an evidentiary hearing it is important to gear up and make sure you are ready. If you have handled your motion pro se up to the granting of the evidentiary hearing your success is commendable. Nevertheless, if at all possible it would be advisable to obtain counsel to represent you at the hearing. As I have previously emphasized, if at all possible it is advisable to obtain counsel who is experienced in the postconviction field. I cannot emphasize enough the need for learned counsel in these proceedings. It is always frustrating for me to come in too late on a person's case and have them tell me that they wish they would have had effective counsel representing them earlier on in the postconviction process.

If you are financially unable to retain private counsel you can still attempt to have counsel appointed by the court. Florida Statutes §924.066(3) does provide that a person in a noncapital case who is seeking collateral review (i.e., postconviction relief) has no statutory right to a court appointed lawyer. However, §924.066(3) does not preclude appointment of counsel when the need for such counsel is plea. See *Russo v. Akers*, 701 So.2d 366 (Fla 5th DCA 1997) [Although there is no absolute right to counsel in a postconviction proceeding, due process requires that counsel be provided if postconviction motion presents a meritorious claim and a hearing on motion is potentially so complex that counsel is necessary]. Thus, counsel should be appointed if a postconviction motion presents a meritorious claim and a hearing on the motion is potentially so complex that counsel is necessary. See *Russo v. Akers*, 724 So.2d 1151 (Fla.1998). Important factors to raise in a motion for appointment of counsel include the adversary nature of the proceeding, its complexity, the need for an evidentiary hearing, or the need for substantial legal research. All of these factors are important elements which may require the appointment of counsel. *Id.*

In addition to the clear benefit of having a trained professional ready to represent you at an evidentiary hearing, there are also other less obvious reasons for obtaining counsel. Firstly, a postconviction movant represented by counsel is more likely than a pro se litigant to get a fair consideration of the issues presented. Secondly, if your counsel is experienced in postconviction matters, he will likely try to negotiate some sort of acceptable outcome with the State prior to ever conducting an evidentiary hearing. While it certainly is not common for the State to come with a new plea agreement prior to an evidentiary hearing, it can and does happen sometimes. Of course, such an outcome depends on any number of factors including how shrewd the attorney is, the strength of the postconviction motion, the laziness of the prosecutor and countless other intangibles. The point is, with experienced counsel there is at least a chance of seeing some sort of relief without ever having to proceed to an evidentiary hearing.

Whether you chose to retain private counsel, ask for appointed counsel, or go it alone, it is advisable that you make sure you are present for any evidentiary hearing of your 3.850. Florida Rule of Criminal procedure 3.850(e) provides that a court may entertain and determine the motion without requiring the presence of the postconviction movant at the evidentiary hearing. While it is within the court's discretion to determine whether a prisoner should be present at a postconviction hearing, this discretion must be exercised with regard to the prisoner's right to due process. *Teffeteller, v Dugger*, 676 So.2d 369 (Fla.1996). The following cases are good examples of circumstances where due process dictates that the presence of the movant is necessary for an evidentiary hearing: *Diggs v. State*, 504 So.2d 792 (Fla 2d DCA 1987)[due process required presence of movant at evidentiary hearing regarding trial counsel's failure to attack credibility of police officer who was a key state witness]; *Smith v. State*, 489 So.2d 197 (Fla.1st DCA 1986)[movant alleging ineffective assistance of counsel was entitled to be present at hearing in which judge examined counsel regarding communications with petitioner prior to entry of guilty plea].

Once you are certain that you will be present for your evidentiary hearing, it is important to begin preparing for the hearing. In some cases it may be beneficial to conduct pre-hearing discovery (i.e., depositions, requests for admissions, etc.). A postconviction movant does not have a guaranteed right to discovery. Nevertheless, on motion for postconviction relief that sets forth good reason, a trial court may allow limited discovery into matters which are relevant and material. *State v. Lewis*, 656 So.2d 1248 (Fla.1994); See also *Davis v. State*, 624 So.2d 282 (Fla. 3rd DCA 1993). Where such discovery is permitted, a trial court may place limitations on the sources and scope. *Id.* In determining whether to allow discovery in a postconviction proceeding, the trial court shall consider the issues presented, the time elapsed between the conviction and postconviction hearing, any burdens imposed on the opposing party and witnesses, alternative means of securing evidence, and any other relevant facts. *Id.*

With regard to pre-hearing discovery, one may wish to take the deposition of his trial counsel. In postconviction cases where the issue is ineffectiveness of counsel, the movant should be allowed to depose trial counsel prior to an evidentiary hearing. See *Davis v. State*, 624 So.2d 282 (Fla 3rd DCA 1993). However, it may not be helpful to take trial counsel's deposition if it is expected that trial counsel's stance will be adversarial to the postconviction movant. Unfortunately, it seems that all too often that trial counsel's own self-interests outweigh any possibility of actually admitting that counsel was ineffective in his representation of the client. If this is expected to be the case, I personally do not like to depose, or even make contact with the trial attorney. By deposing an adversarial trial attorney, you are actually giving trial counsel a 'dress rehearsal' and giving said attorney the opportunity to contrive plausible reasons for ineffective conduct. I personally prefer to catch such adversarial attorneys off guard at the actual evidentiary hearing when I know that they are going to deny a claim of ineffective representation. Of course, determining whether or not to depose trial counsel is a case by case decision and must be decided by taking the individual trial attorney's personality, relationship with the former client, and stance on the issues presented in the 3.850 into account.

If you are handling your evidentiary hearing pro se, make sure you are prepared to back up any issues you present both with the necessary evidence and applicable case law. Do not count on the court to assist you in formulating an argument. Prior to the hearing, try to anticipate what the State's response will be and how you can destroy that State's claims. It is helpful to have other people try to poke holes in your claims so that you will know how to defend against such arguments at the evidentiary hearing. It is also advisable to be familiar with all applicable case law and be ready to argue to the court why such cases apply to your situation. Obviously it is preferable to have an attorney do these things for you, but if you cannot afford an attorney and the court refuses to appoint one, you need to be ready to present your case the best that you can. Finally, be aware that by raising claims of ineffective assistance of counsel, you are waiving your attorney/client privilege as it relates to the attorney under attack. *Arbelaez v. State*, 775 So.2d 909 (Fla. 2000). Therefore, if there are matters that may be detrimental to your claims (such as an admission of guilt to the attorney) it is likely that such matters may be testified to at the evidentiary hearing.

Do not expect that the trial court will make a decision on your postconviction claims immediately at the conclusion of the evidentiary hearing. Often, a court will reserve its ruling until it is able to further research case law, trial transcripts, court records, et cetera. If this is the case, it may be helpful to present supplemental arguments and/or case authority to the court. Be careful with any supplemental argument, though, that you do not merely reargue points that have already been clearly made. It does not help to overload the court with unnecessary pleadings and may delay rendition of a final order on your 3.850. Therefore, use your opportunity to supplement your argument carefully and only when it seems that the court did not understand an important point.

Finally, if your 3.850 is denied after an evidentiary hearing, do not give up. You still have the right to appeal such a denial of relief. In my next article I intend to explain the appellate process after the denial of a 3.850.

3.850 APPEALS

Up to this point in my articles I have been tracking the typical progression of a postconviction attack on a judgment and sentence via a Rule 3.850 Motion for Postconviction Relief. On the road to relief there are usually numerous hurdles to clear before any type of relief is granted. One such hurdle is merely obtaining an evidentiary hearing on the claims presented in a 3.850. Since courts are often reluctant to grant convicted persons well-deserved relief, the trial courts will deny meritorious claims after an evidentiary hearing. The postconviction litigant is once again forced to rely on the district courts of appeal in order to continue fighting his conviction. This article focuses on the appellate process that follows when a 3.850 has been denied after an evidentiary hearing.

If a postconviction case makes it to an evidentiary hearing and then is denied, the case is not necessarily dead at that time. There is still the right to appeal the trial court's judgment. In order to commence an appeal after the denial of a 3.850 (with evidentiary hearing), the original notice of appeal, as well as one copy, must be filed with the trial court within 30 days of the date of the order denying relief. See Florida Rule of Appellate Procedure (hereinafter *FRAP*) 9.110(b). A sample Notice of Appeal form is provided in *FRAP* 9.900(a).

Additionally, since there has already been an evidentiary hearing held, it will be important to prepare a designation to the court reporter informing the court reporter to transcribe the evidentiary hearing. For the *pro se* petitioner, the notice of appeal (after the evidentiary hearing), in and of itself acts to direct the court reporter to transcribe the evidentiary hearing. *FRAP* 9.141(b)(3)(A). Nevertheless, I would still advise a *pro se* appellant to prepare a Designation to Reporter listing any hearings (and their dates) that need to be transcribed for the record on the appeal. Do not leave it up to the clerk of court or anybody else to protect your rights and make sure the record is properly prepared. The Designation to Reporter must be filed with the trial court and provided to the court reporter within 10 days of the filing of the notice of appeal. See, *FRAP* 9.200(b). *FRAP* 9.900(h) provides a sample form for the Designation to Reporter.

Upon filing notice of appeal, the circuit court clerk will begin preparing the record on appeal. Unless otherwise requested, the record on the appeal will consist of the notice of appeal, the 3.850, the court's order on the motion, any motion for rehearing and responses to said motion, and the transcript of the evidentiary hearing. *FRAP* 9.141(b)(3)(B)(i). Often though, the record on appeal that is automatically prepared by the clerk of court will be insufficient to give the appellate court a full picture of what may have happened with the litigant's claims. In fact, unless it is requested, the clerk of the circuit court will not include discovery documents, subpoenas, and/or depositions in the record on the appeal. See *FRAP* 9.200(a). And, if crucial documents are not included in the record on appeal, they cannot be referred to or relied upon. In fact, an omission of important documents could cause an appeal to be lost. "Even where an appeal might have merit, the failure to adhere to the record on appeal can be fatal." *Gladstone v. Smith*, 729 So.2d 1002 (Fla. 4th DCA 1999). Therefore, if I am ever in doubt as to whether something important will automatically be included in the record on appeal, I always make sure to prepare directions to the clerk of court, informing the clerk of the documents that need to be included in the record on appeal. *FRAP* 9.9000(g) provides a sample form for the Directions to Clerk.

Once the notice of appeal has been filed, the clerk of circuit court is supposed to prepare the record on appeal and transmit the record to the district court within 50 days. *FRAP* 9.141(b)(3)(B)(i). Often the trial courts are not timely in their preparation of the record on appeal. This may be because of mistakes made by the clerk, because the court reporter has not timely prepared a transcript, or for any other number of reasons. Regardless, the appellant will have 30 days from the date of the service of the record on appeal (or its index), to file the Initial Brief. *FRAP* 9.141(b)(3)(C).

It is true that a *pro se* postconviction petitioner's pleadings will not be held to the technical standards set forth for attorneys. *Andrews v. State*, So. 2d726 (Fla. 3rd DCA 1964) [" . . . it must always be borne in mind that such motions filed by a prisoner *pro se* should not be scrutinized for technical niceties, since a prisoner is almost always unskilled in the law and cannot be held to a high standard of pleading."] Nevertheless, the closer one follows the Rules of Appellate Procedure, the more professional the pleadings will be. A more professional initial brief certainly cannot hurt one's case and is more likely to help the appellate court understand the issues. Thus, it is important for the *pro se* appellant to be familiar with the rules regarding the required brief formats. *FRAP* 9.210 sets forth the pleading requirements for appellate briefs.

Inmates may have an inability to type their pleadings and may have to present their briefs to the courts in handwritten form. If the appellate briefs will be typed, though, the lettering should (if possible) be black, double-spaced, and with margins of no less than one inch. *FRAP* 9.210(a)(2). If the brief is computer generated, they should be submitted in Times New Roman 14-point font or Courier New 12 point font. *FRAP* 9.210, Additionally, the courts now require that appellate briefs include a certificate of type size and font at the end of the briefs indicating that they have been prepared with the proper font. Finally, the Initial Brief should not exceed fifty pages unless the appellate court has granted permission to exceed the fifty page limit. It is advisable, before preparing your Initial Brief, to review all requirements set forth in *FRAP* 9.210.

FRAP 9.210(b) sets forth the requirements for the Initial Brief. The Initial Brief must include: (1) a table of contents with references to page numbers; (2) a table of citations containing page references with the cases listed alphabetically and referring to any other statutes or legal authorities cited in the brief; (3) a statement of the case and facts with citations to the record; (4) a short (usually not more than 2 pages) summary of the argument; (5) argument with regard to each issue presented; and (6) a conclusion of not more than one page setting forth the precise relief sought.

Hopefully the foregoing article has been helpful to *pro se* petitioners who are currently appealing an improper denial of a 3.850. I would recommend that any person representing himself in such a matter thoroughly familiarize himself with the Florida Rules of Appellate Procedure (particularly the rules mentioned in this article). Although the *pro se* petitioner will not be held to the same technical pleading requirements that attorneys are held to, it is still a good practice to try to make your brief as professional looking as possible.

JUDICIAL ESTOPPEL

Often when a 3.850 Motion makes it to the stage of an evidentiary hearing, it seems that the State will take whatever position is necessary to refute the movant's claims. Sometimes this means that the State will take a position that is directly in conflict with its previous position at trial or on appeal. It is improper and unethical for a prosecutor to do this. Unfortunately, though, it happens often enough that one should be prepared for such a tactic at an evidentiary hearing. When the State tries to switch arguments on an issue at a postconviction evidentiary hearing, one should be ready to argue the doctrine of judicial estoppel to prevent such an unfair and opportunistic attempt to refute claims.

In Florida, the general rule of judicial estoppel is that a claim or position successfully maintained in a former action or judicial proceeding bars a party from making a completely inconsistent claim or taking a clearly conflicting position in a subsequent action or judicial proceeding, to the prejudice of the adverse party, where the parties are the same in both actions. *Grau v. Provident Life and Acc. Ins. Co.*, 899 So.2d 396 (2005); See also *Federated Mut. Implement and Hardware Ins. Co. v. Griffin*, 237 So.2d 38 (Fla. 1st DCA, 1970) [litigants are not permitted to take inconsistent positions in judicial proceedings, and a party cannot allege one state of facts for one purpose and at the same action or proceeding deny such allegations and set up a new and different state of facts inconsistent thereto for another purpose].

The doctrine of judicial estoppel has been developed to protect the integrity of the judicial process and to prevent parties from "making a mockery of justice by inconsistent pleadings." *Grau quoting American National Bank v. Federal Deposit Ins. Corp.*, 710 F.2d 1528, 1536 (11th Cir. 1983). Judicial estoppel further prevents parties from "playing fast and loose with the courts." *Russell v. Rolfs*, 893 F.2d 1033, 1037 (9th Cir. 1990). A situation justifying the application of judicial estoppel "is more than affront to judicial dignity. For intentional self-contradiction is being used as a means of obtaining unfair advantage in a forum provided for suitors seeking justice." *Scarano v. Cen. R. Co. of N.J.*, 203 F.2nd 510, 513 (3rd Cir. 1953).

Thus, if a prosecutor argues an issue one way at trial and then later takes the opposite position at a postconviction evidentiary hearing, he should be judicially estopped from using the intentional self-contradiction as a means of obtaining an unfair advantage at the evidentiary hearing. Even if the prosecutor at the evidentiary hearing is different from the original prosecutor on the case, he still should not be able to argue a position which conflicts with the one which the State previously presented at trial or on appeal. Any State Attorney's office is the equivalent of a law firm and should be bound by the arguments (either factual or legal) previously made by another assistant state attorney. Being prepared with the above case-law is the best way to prevent the State from making a mockery of justice through the use of inconsistent positions.

BELATED APPEAL

The focus of many of my previous articles has been on a motion for postconviction relief that is filed pursuant to Rule 3.850. As Rule 3.850 is probably the most used postconviction vehicle, it makes sense for someone who is researching his postconviction case to dedicate a substantial amount of time to an attack pursuant to said rule. However, an often overlooked and worthwhile postconviction possibility is an attack on the appellate process via a Florida Rule of Appellate Procedure 9.141(c) Petition for Writ of Habeas Corpus alleging ineffectiveness of appellate counsel.

In the State of Florida a defendant has a right under the Florida Constitution to pursue a direct appeal from a trial court's imposition of a judgment and sentence. *See* Art. V., §4(B), Florida Constitution. And, where a state provides for a direct appeal as a matter of right (as Florida has done), a criminal defendant has a right to counsel to help prosecute his appeal. *Douglas v. California*, 372 U.S. 353 (1963); and, *State v. Weeks*, 166 So.2d 892 (Fla. 1966). Most importantly, the right to appellate counsel is the right to effective assistance of such counsel. *Evitts v. Lucy*, 469 U.S. 387 (1985).

Florida Rule of Appellate Procedure 9.141(c) provides the authority for a petition for writ of habeas corpus alleging ineffective assistance of appellate counsel. The 9.141(c) petition must be filed with the appellate court to which the direct appeal was or should have been taken. As with Rule 3.850, a 9.141(c) petition has a period of limitations. A petition for belated appeal alleging ineffectiveness of appellate counsel must be filed within two years of when the conviction in question becomes final. The only way around the two-year period of limitations is if the petitioner alleges, under oath, that he was affirmatively misled about the results of the appeal by appellate counsel. Florida Rule of Appellate Procedure 9.141(c)(5)(A).

A rule 9.141 petition must provide the following:

♦   The date and nature of the lower court's order to be reviewed
♦   The name of the lower court rendering the order
♦   The nature, disposition, and dates of all previous proceedings in the lower tribunal and, if any, appellate courts
♦   if a previous petition for a belated appeal was filed, the reason the claim in the present petition was not raised previously
♦   the nature of the relief sought, and
♦   the specific acts sworn to by the petitioner that constitute the alleged ineffective assistance of counsel

Typically the relief that will be requested is a belated appeal whereby the petitioner can raise an appellate issue that could, and should, have been raised in the original direct appeal. Therefore, the issue to be raised in a petition for writ of habeas corpus alleging ineffectiveness of appellate counsel is that counsel was ineffective for failing to raise a meritorious issue. *Groover v. Singletary*, 656 So.2d 424 (Fla. 1995). The actual legal issue that was not raised on appeal is only relevant to determine whether the petitioner should be afforded the opportunity to present that issue in a belated appeal. *Rogers v. State*, 698 So. 2d 1178 (Fla. 1996).

As with ineffectiveness of trial counsel claims, the test for ineffectiveness of appellate counsel is a two-pronged test where both ineffectiveness and prejudice to the petitioner must be established. Thus, to determine whether appellate counsel was ineffective, the appellate court's evaluation is limited to: "first, whether the alleged omissions are of such magnitude as to constitute a serious error or substantial deficiency falling measurably outside the range of professionally acceptable performance and, second, whether the deficiency in performance compromised the appellate process to such a degree as to undermine confidence in the correctness of the result." *Groover v. Singletary,* 656 So.2d 424, 425 (Fla. 1995).

Once a petition alleging ineffectiveness of appellate counsel is filed, the appellate court will often issue an Order to Show Cause to the State directing the State to reply to the petition. Often the State will reply, without any supporting evidence, that appellate counsel should not be deemed ineffective for choosing to pursue other stronger appellate arguments in lieu of the one that counsel is alleged to have been ineffective for omitting. *See Julius v. Johnson,* 840 F.2d 1533 (11th Cir. 1988). This is a veiled strategy argument that can be rebutted on several fronts. Firstly, if the issue to be raised goes to the heart of the case, the appellate court needs to be made aware of the importance of the issue. An issue that is crucial to the validity of the conviction and goes to the heart of the case " . . . cannot be excused as mere strategy or allocation of appellate resources." *Wilson v. Wainwright,* 474 So.2d 1162 (Fla. 1985). Additionally, it is important to point out to the court that a court's finding that some action or inaction by counsel was tactical is generally inappropriate without an evidentiary hearing. *See, Thomas v. State,* 634 So.2d 1157 (Fla.1st. DCA 1994).

If the appellate court determines that the petitioner has demonstrated both ineffectiveness of appellate counsel and resulting prejudice, then a belated appeal will likely be granted. At that point the petitioner will then be able to pursue the issue that was previously omitted from his or her original direct appeal and the rules of appellate procedure will all apply to any further proceedings. Hopefully this article has added another angle of attack for some people who were previously unaware of Rule 9.141(c). Rule 9.141(c) may or may not be something that is helpful, depending on the case, but it is always something worth looking into when one is researching postconviction options.

FEDERAL PETITION for WRIT of HABEAS CORPUS

My previous articles have addressed potential state postconviction remedies for incarcerated persons. The state remedies are the most likely to obtain postconviction relief for convicted persons. Nevertheless, another important vehicle for obtaining postconviction relief is the Title 28 United States Code (U.S.C.) §2254 federal petition for writ of habeas corpus. Essentially, the 2254 petition allows the state inmate to present his constitutional claims to the federal courts. Unfortunately, though, since the Antiterrorism and Effective Death Penalty Act of 1996 (AEDPA) was passed, federal postconviction relief for state prisoners has become exceedingly more difficult to obtain. The AEDPA is apparently misnamed as it does not only affect terrorists and death sentences. It affects every state prisoner who wishes to rely on the federal courts for postconviction relief. And, if one does not have sufficient knowledge regarding the AEDPA, he may end up waiving his right to pursue such relief in the federal courts.

The AEDPA imposes numerous requirements before the merits of a §2254 petition will even be considered by the federal courts. Firstly, as with 3.850 motions, there is a period of limitations which can bar consideration of a 2254 petition. Title 28 U.S.C. §2244(d)(1) provides a one-year period of limitation for filing the federal petition. The period of limitation shall begin running from the latest of the following:

(1)   The date on which the judgment became final by the
      conclusion of direct review or the expiration of the time for
      seeking such review;

(2)   The date on which the impediment to filing an application
      created by State action, in violation of the Constitution or
      laws of the United States, is removed, if the applicant was
      prevented from filing by such State action;

(3)   The date on which the constitutional right asserted was
      initially recognized by the United States Supreme Court, if
      the right has been newly recognized by the Supreme Court
      and made retroactively applicable to cases on collateral
      review; or,

(4)   The date on which the factual predicate of the claim or
      claims could have been discovered through the exercise of
      due diligence.

The first starting date for the running of the one-year period of limitations, the date on which the judgment became final, is likely going to be the starting date for most inmates. In this case, the one-year federal period of limitations begins 90 days after the conclusion of your direct appeal and any rehearings filed thereon. It is important to understand that the 90 days (a period for filing for United State Supreme Court certiorari) is calculated from the final order affirming the judgment and sentence (and not from the later date on which the appellate court issues the Mandate on the appeal). Alternatively, if you entered a plea and did not appeal your judgment and sentence, your conviction would be final 120 days after the imposition of the sentence (30 days for the filing of the notice of appeal, plus the 90 day period for filing for Supreme Court certiorari). See *Gonzalez v. Thaler*, 132 S.Ct. 641 (2012), for discussion on the 90-day period for certiorari and its effect of tolling the one-year federal period of limitations. By using the above starting dates, you will ensure that your federal 2254 petition is timely filed.

When the AEDPA first became effective there was some confusion as to whether the one-year period of limitations began to run after the collateral attacks were final. This was so because Florida provides a two-year period of limitations for filing the state postconviction motion. I have personally reviewed many cases where the habeas petitioners timely filed a 3.850 motion within the state courts prior to the end of state two-year period of limitations but after the federal one-year period of limitations had run. Those people were procedurally barred from pursuing federal relief. Your federal one-year period of limitations begins running at the time your Judgment and Sentence is final, *not* when your state collateral postconviction proceedings are final.

It is important to realize, though, that the AEDPA does provide a tolling provision for the time period that your state postconviction motions are *properly* filed. Title 28 U.S.C. §2244(d)(1) provides that "[t]he time during which a properly filed application for State postconviction or other collateral review with respect to the pertinent judgment or claim is pending shall not be counted toward any period of limitation under this section." Thus, the time stops running on the one-year period of limitation during the time which a state collateral postconviction motion is *properly filed*, and does not begin to run again until the conclusion of said collateral motion, including the appeal therefrom. It is important to keep in mind that the state claims must be properly filed, in the proper court, in order to toll the federal one-year period of limitations. For example, if a claim of ineffective assistance of appellate counsel is asserted in the improper vehicle of a 3.850 motion (it should be raised in a petition for writ of habeas corpus to the appellate court), and is denied because it was filed in the wrong court, the time during which that motion was filed does not serve to toll the federal period of limitations because the motion was not "properly filed."

A Florida Rule of Criminal Procedure 3.850 Motion that is timely filed, and which asserts the proper claims, does serve to toll the running of the federal one-year period of limitations. This is important because the Title 28 U.S.C. §2254 (b)(1)(A) also requires that the habeas petitioner must have first exhausted his constitutional claims in the state court. While the State can expressly waive the exhaustion requirement and allow unexhausted claims to be reviewed by the federal court [See §2254(c)], for all practical purposes this will almost never happen. Therefore it is important to make sure that you have exhausted your claims in the state courts before seeking federal relief. As a general rule, the habeas corpus petitioner will have satisfied the exhaustion requirement if the claim is presented to the proper state court as is required by the applicable state law, thus giving the state court " . . . meaningful opportunity to consider the allegations of legal error." *Vasquez v. Hillery*, 474 U.S. 254 (1986).

It is extremely important that all claims raised in a 2254 petition be exhausted at the state level prior to submitting the claims in the federal petition. If a 2254 petition is a "mixed petition" which contains both exhausted and unexhausted issues, the federal district court can dismiss the petition, without prejudice, so that the petitioner can exhaust the unexhausted claims at the state level. See *Rose v. Lundy*, 455 U.S. 509 (1982). If the petition is dismissed, the one-year period of limitations often expires before the petitioner has had the opportunity to exhaust the petition at the state level and then reassert the claims in a new 2254 petition. Of course if you have filed a mixed petition, you may wish to ask the federal court to hold your petition in abeyance while the unexhausted claims are pursued at the state level. While the federal circuits are split on whether this is proper, there is authority to support such a request. See *Zarvela v. Artuz*, 254 F.3d 374 (2d Cir. 2001) [after dismissing the unexhausted claims of a mixed petition a district court should exercise discretion to either to stay further proceedings on the remaining portion of the petition or to dismiss the petition in its entirety]. In *Zarvela* the Second Circuit Court of Appeals for the United States held that " . . . in many cases, a stay will be preferable . . . and . . . will be the only appropriate course in cases . . . where an outright dismissal 'could jeopardize the timeliness of a collateral attack." Therefore, there is the possibility that a federal district court may hold a mixed petition in abeyance until the unexhausted issues are finalized at the state level. Nevertheless, it is advisable to first fully exhaust all claims prior to filing a 2254 petition in order to avoid the possibility of a mixed petition being dismissed in its entirety.

In my next article I will continue to address the filing of a §2254 petition for writ of habeas corpus in more detail. In the meantime, I recommend that anyone who may be interested in filing such a petition be aware of the one-year period of limitations as it applies to your case and make sure that you do not let that time lapse. Additionally, any persons who will be handling their 2254 petitions *pro se* should further familiarize themselves with the complexities involved in the federal litigation. Of course, if at all possible I recommend that potential federal habeas petitioners retain experienced counsel for their federal habeas pursuits. But, if that simply is not a reality, I recommend a thorough review of Lexis Publishing's *Federal Habeas Corpus Practice and Procedure, 6th Edition,* by James S. Liebman and Randy Hertz. Said book is an excellent guide to anyone undertaking the task of pursuing a federal 2254 petition.

PREPARATION and FILING of §2254 PETITION

Before filing a Title 28 §2254 petition for writ of habeas, it is best to review the local rules of the federal district court before which you will be filing your petition. There are three federal districts in Florida: the northern, the middle and the southern districts. While each district court is bound by the Federal Rules of Civil Procedure (a 2254 petition is civil in nature, not criminal), each district also has local rules that must be followed. And, each district's local rules can differ. For example, the Northern District requires that a 2254 petition be prepared on the form provided in the Appendix of Forms to the Rules Governing Sections 2254 Cases, while the Middle District does not impose such a requirement. There are many slight differences in the requirements of the local rules so it is always advisable to review said rules and make sure that your federal habeas petition complies with the Rules of Civil Procedure and the local rules of your federal court. If you do not have the local rules readily available, then you should write the clerk of your district court and request a copy of said rules.

The Appendix to the Rules Governing Section 2254 Cases in the United States District Courts provides a Model Form for a §2254 habeas corpus petition. Said form will be extremely helpful to the *pro se* petitioner as it informs the petitioner all of the information the district court will need in order to consider the petition. It is not necessary to cite case law in your petition itself. Instead, I would recommend that a memorandum in support of your petition be filed which fleshes out your claims with supporting case law and application of the legal standards to the facts of your case.

It is important to plan your petition out ahead of time and make sure that you raise all of your issues in one petition. You will want to raise all of the constitutional issues that you have already presented in your direct appeal and state postconviction motion(s). If you try to present several habeas corpus petitions, which attack the same judgment and sentence, any petitions after your first one will likely be considered successive. In order to file a second or successive 2254 petition, authorization for filing such a petition must be obtained from the Eleventh Circuit Court of Appeals. See 28 U.S.C. § 2244(b)(3). Authorization forms may be obtained from the applicable district court or the Eleventh Circuit.

When you file your 2254 petition, it is very possible that it will be assigned to a magistrate judge instead of a federal district court judge. Title 28 U.S.C. §636 (b)(1)(A) authorizes the district judge in habeas corpus cases to appoint a magistrate judge to consider your 2254 petition. While the magistrate judge does not have the power to render a final and binding decision on your case, he will submit to the court proposed findings of fact and a recommendation for a disposition of your case. Once a report and recommendation is issued by the magistrate judge, the parties to the case have 14 days from the date of the report to file objections with the district judge. If such objections are filed, the objecting party may receive a *de novo* review of the petition. As is provided in Rule 8(b)(4) of the Rules Governing Section 2254 Cases in the United States District Courts: "The judge must determine *de novo* any proposed finding or recommendation to which objection is made. The judge may accept, reject, or modify any proposed finding or recommendation." Therefore, if there is a report and recommendation from a magistrate judge in your case, then any harmful aspects of the report and recommendation should be objected to within fourteen days. In addition to obtaining a *de novo* review of the issues, this also serves to preserve your objections for appeal. Generally, in the Eleventh Circuit Court of Appeals for the United States, a petitioner must object to the magistrate's report and recommendation in order to preserve the issue for appeal. Thus, it is the best practice to always file written objections to the magistrate's report. It will obtain a *de novo* review of the issues and facts, and will preserve your right to pursue your appeal if necessary.

There are numerous issues that can be raised in a 2254 petition. Of course, as was discussed in my last article, it is very important that you first exhaust these issues at the state level before raising them in your 2254 petition. Because the potential issues that can be raised in a 2254 are so varied, there is no possible way I could provide an exhaustive list of such claims. Therefore, I will merely try to give some examples that I hope will be helpful. Of course the best places to look for issues to present in your 2254 petition are in your direct appeal and any state postconviction motions that you have filed. Any issues of a constitutional (federal constitution) nature that have previously been raised will be ripe for consideration in your 2254 petition. The following are examples of issues are cognizable in 2254 proceedings:

- *Jury Instructions- Thomas v. Kemp*, 800 F. 2d 1024 (11th Cir., 1986); and, *Drake v. Kemp*, 762 F.2d 1449 (11th Cir. 1985).
- *Counsel's Failure to Investigate Case- Futch v. Dugger*, 874 F.2d 1483 (11th Cir. 1989); *Aldrich v. Wainwright*, 777 F.2d 630 (11th Cir. 1985); and, *Code v. Montgomery*, 799 F.2d 1481 (11th Cir. 1986).
- *Ineffective Assistance of Counsel- Strickland v. Washington*, 466 U.S. 668 (1984); and, *Smith v. Dugger*, 911 F.2d 494 (11th Cir. 1990).
- *Ineffectiveness of Appellate Counsel- Evitts v. Lucey-* 469 U.S. 387 (1985); and, *Mayo v. Henderson*, 13 F.3d 528 (2nd Cir. 1994).
- *Prosecutorial Misconduct- Troedel v. Dugger*, 828 F.2d 670 (11th Cir. 1987); and, *Brown v. Wainwright*, 785 F.2d 1457 (11th Cir. 1986).
- *Issues Relating to the Defendant's Competency to Stand Trial- Wallace v. Kemp*, 757 F.2d 1102 (11th Cir. 1985); and

Strickland v. Francisu, 738 F.2d 1542 (11th Cir. 1984).

- ◆ *Issues relating Jury Selection-* See, *Amadeo v. Zant*, 486 U.S.
  214 (1988); and *Coleman v. Kemp*, 778 F.2d 1487 (11th Cir.
  1985).

- • *Involuntary Statements to Law Enforcement- Christopher v.
  Florida*, 824 F2d 836 (11th Cir.1987); and, *Cervi v. Kemp*,
  855 F.2d 702 (11th Cir. 1988).

- ◆ *Claims Relating to Involuntary Pleas- U.S. v. Loughery*, 908
  F.2d 1014 (D.C. Cir. 1990); and, *Garmon v. Lockhart*, 938
  F.2d 120 (8th Cir. 1991).

There are many more issues that can be raised in a 2254 petition, therefore, I recommend that you not limit yourself to the above issues. I also recommend that you not fall into the trap of thinking you did not preserve your constitutional issues at the state level because only state law was referenced in your briefs or motions. Just because federal case law was not cited, it does not mean that you did not raise the constitutional issue in the state courts. As long as the constitutional question was addressed, then your issue was raised and exhausted, and is ripe for federal review.

In my next issue I will be addressing the appeal from the denial of a 2254 petition and the pursuit of a certificate of appealability for permission to appeal your case. In the meantime I wish my readers good luck with their postconviction pursuits.

§2254 APPEALS

My most recent articles have dealt with the filing of a U.S.C. Title 28 §2254 petition for writ of habeas corpus with the federal district courts. Unfortunately, since the Antiterrorism and Effective Death Penalty Act of 1996 (AEDPA) was passed, it has become extremely difficult for state prisoners to obtain collateral relief from a judgment and/or sentence in the federal courts. The likelihood is that a federal 2254 habeas petition will be denied at the district court level. Unlike at the state level, the petitioner does not automatically have the right to appeal the denial of a 2254 petition. This article will deal with initiating an appeal of the denial of a §2254 petition and requesting a certificate of appealability in order to obtain permission to pursue an appeal.

Once a district court has issued an order denying a §2254 petition, the habeas petitioner has several options. Firstly, the petitioner can file a postjudgment motion asking the district court to reconsider the denial of the §2254 petition. Federal Rules of Civil Procedure 52(b), 59, and 60 all provide vehicles for filing such postjudgment motions. Federal Rule of Civil Procedure 52(b) provides that "[o]n a party's motion filed no later than 28 days after the entry of judgment, the court may amend its findings--or make additional findings--and may amend the judgment accordingly." Therefore, if the petitioner wishes to request rehearing or reconsideration of the denial of a §2254 petition, a motion should be filed requesting such reconsideration within 28 days of the order denying relief. Such a post-trial motion should usually be filed pursuant to Federal Rule of Civil Procedure 52(b) and should be presented in the form of a *Motion to Alter or Amend Judgment.*

It is not necessary to file a *Motion to Alter or Amend Judgment* in order to pursue an appeal of the denial of a §2254 petition. The filing of such a motion, though, does toll (stop) the running of the jurisdictional period for filing a notice of appeal. *See,* Federal Rule of Appellate Procedure 4(A)(4)(a)(ii). The decision whether to file a *Motion to Alter or Amend Judgment* or other appropriate postjudgment motion is a judgment call on the part of the petitioner. It has been my experience that once a federal district court denies a §2254 petition, it is unlikely that a postjudgment motion requesting reconsideration will be granted by the same judge. Nevertheless, the right to file such a motion does exist, and, as long as it is timely filed, does not jeopardize the ability to file a notice of appeal in a timely manner. I recommend that before filing such a postjudgment motion, though, that the petitioner determine whether he is willing to accept the additional delay of the appellate process that will follow. If such a delay is acceptable, then there is no harm done by filing a *Motion to Alter or Amend Judgment* or other appropriate postjudgment motion.

Generally, once a court has entered a final order on a §2254 petition, the petitioner has 30 days therefrom to file a *Notice of Appeal* if an appeal is to be pursued. *See,* Federal Rule of Appellate Procedure 4(a)(1). The requirements for a *Notice of Appeal* are listed in Federal Rule of Appellate Procedure 3(c) and a *Notice of Appeal* form is provided in Form 1 of the Appendix of Forms to the Federal Rules of Appellate Procedure. If a *Motion to Alter or Amend Judgment* or other appropriate postjudgment motion has been timely filed, then the 30-day period for filing the *Notice of Appeal* begins running from the date of the entry of a final order disposing of said motion. *See,* Federal Rule of Appellate Procedure 4(a)(4). Otherwise, if no such postjudgment motion has been filed, the 30-day period for filing of the *Notice of Appeal* begins running from the date of the final order on the §2254 petition.

Once a *Notice of Appeal* has been filed, it does not automatically mean the petitioner is allowed to appeal the district court's denial of relief. Unlike many other litigants in the federal courts, habeas corpus petitioners must obtain permission to take an appeal of their case to the circuit court of appeals. The permission to appeal must be granted by either the district court or the circuit court of appeals. Said permission is granted in the form of a *Certificate of Appealability* (hereinafter, *COA*). *See*, Federal Rule of Appellate Procedure 22(b)(1).

Title 28 U.S.C. Section 2253(c)(2) provides that a certificate of appealability will be issued only if the applicant "has made a substantial showing of the denial of a constitutional right." Furthermore, in *Barefoot v. Estelle*, 463 U.S. 880 (1983), the U.S. Supreme Court held that in order for a certificate of probable cause (the pre-AEDPA equivalent of the current Certificate of Appealability) to be issued the appellant must make a "substantial showing of the denial of [a] federal right." In defining the "substantial showing" standard, the Supreme Court admonished district courts that they may not deny applications for probable cause certificates solely because they have already denied the petition on the merits: "[O]bviously the petitioner need not show that he should prevail on the merits. He has already failed in that endeavor." *Id.* at 893.

The U.S. Supreme Court held that rather, a certificate must issue if the appeal presents a "question of some substance," i.e., at least one issue: (1) that is "debatable among jurists of reason"; (2) "that a court could resolve in a different manner"; (3) that is "adequate to deserve encouragement to proceed further"; or, (4) that is not "squarely foreclosed by statute, rule or authoritative court decision, or [that is not] lacking any factual basis in the record." *Barefoot* at 893. It has been held, in *Hardwick v. Singletary*, 126 F.3d 1312 (11th Cir 1997), that the standard governing certificates of appealability for appeal of the denial of a habeas corpus petition under the AEDPA is materially identical to the pre-AEDPA standard for certificates of probable cause for the appeal of a denial of a habeas corpus petition.

Therefore, in an *Application for Certificate of Appealability*, it is crucial for the applicant to demonstrate a substantial showing of the denial of a federal right. The factors listed in *Barefoot* must be sufficiently argued and applied to the applicant's case in order to obtain a *COA*. While it is likely that the district judge who denied a §2254 petition will also deny an *Application for Certificate of Appealability*, it is still recommendable that the habeas petitioner file such an application. And, if the district court denies a request for a *COA*, Federal Rule of Criminal Procedure 22(b) also provides for the issuance of a *COA* by the circuit court of appeals. While it is rare that permission to appeal the denial of a §2254 petition is granted, *COA*'s are occasionally issued and petitioners do sometimes pursue appeals to the federal circuit courts of appeals. I hope that this article has been helpful in pointing habeas corpus petitioners in the right direction when attempting to obtain a *COA*.

BELATED 3.850 PETITIONS

Often when one is considering pursuing postconviction relief from a criminal conviction, the person is quite likely going to make allegations of ineffective assistance of trial or appellate counsel. Of course each and every person charged with a crime has a constitutional right, pursuant to the Sixth Amendment of the U.S. Constitution, to effective assistance of counsel. *Strickland v. Washington*, 466 U.S. 668 (1984). Likewise, a person already convicted of a crime has the constitutional right to effective assistance of appellate counsel. *Evitts v. Lucy*, 469 U.S. 387 (1985); *Cuyler v. Sullivan*, 446 U.S. 335 (1980). Unfortunately, though, the right to effective assistance of counsel generally does not extend to the right to effective collateral/postconviction counsel. And, even more unfortunately, convicted persons often turn for help to attorneys who are not experienced in the postconviction field. As such, many postconviction litigants are denied effective representation of counsel. While there is generally not much that can be done about ineffective representation rendered by a postconviction attorney, there are certain circumstances where the mistakes of postconviction attorneys can be collaterally attacked. Often when an attorney is not experienced with postconviction cases, the attorney will fail to timely file a postconviction motion or an appeal therefrom. The focus of this article is the remedying of such a failure on the part of an ineffective attorney so that the postconviction litigant may have an untimely postconviction motion reinstated and considered on its merits.

I have run across many cases where a person had legitimate postconviction claims and he unfortunately hired an attorney unfamiliar with the Rules of Criminal Procedure as they pertain to postconviction cases. While the person might have had meritorious claims, his attorney failed to file a postconviction motion within the two-year period of limitations provided in Florida Rule of Criminal Procedure 3.850. If a 3.850 motion is untimely filed, the trial court will deny the motion because it is filed outside of the period of limitations. But, if the untimeliness of the motion is due to the failure or negligence of retained postconviction counsel, the chances are good that one can get his 3.850 motion reinstated.

Firstly, it is important to note that a criminal defendant does not have a due process right, pursuant to the Sixth Amendment of the U.S. Constitution, to effective assistance of counsel in a postconviction proceeding. *Lambrix v. State*, 698 So.2d 247 (Fla. 1996). However, the holding of *Lambrix* does not dictate that a postconviction movant is to receive no due process whatsoever. In fact, it was held in *State v. Weeks*, 166 So.2d 892 (Fla. 1964), that "[postconviction] remedies are subject to the more flexible standards of due process announced in the Fifth Amendment, Constitution of the United States." *Weeks* at 896. For example, in *Weeks* and *Graham v. State*, 372 So.2d 1363 (Fla. 1979), the Florida Supreme Court held that due process required the appointment of postconviction counsel when a prisoner filed a substantially meritorious postconviction motion and a hearing on the motion was potentially so complex that the assistance of counsel was needed. Thus, although a postconviction movant may not have the right to effective postconviction counsel pursuant to the Sixth Amendment of the United States Constitution, said movant shall still be afforded the more flexible standards of due process.

The Florida Supreme Court recognized the more flexible standard of due process in *Steele v. Kehoe*, 747 So.2d 931 (Fla. 1999). In *Steele*, William Steele was convicted of first-degree murder and sentenced to life in prison. Steele claimed that he retained an attorney to file a motion for postconviction relief pursuant to Florida Rule of Criminal Procedure 3.850, and that said attorney orally agreed to file a motion for postconviction relief. Steele's attorney failed to file a postconviction motion in a timely manner. Steele then filed a rule 3.850 motion on his own. The motions were rejected by the trial court and the court of appeal affirmed the rejection because the motions were filed after the two-year deadline had expired. Ultimately, the Florida Supreme Court held that " . . . due process entitles a prisoner to a hearing on a claim that he or she missed the deadline to file a rule 3.850 motion because his or her attorney had agreed to file the motion but failed to do so in a timely manner." *Id.* As such, the *Steele* Court held that the correct procedure would be for the trial court to conduct a hearing on whether the attorney undertook to file a 3.850 motion on Steele's behalf, but failed to timely file the motion. And, if such circumstances are proven, then the right to file a belated 3.850 motion should be granted. Pursuant to *Steele*, Florida Rule of Criminal Procedure 3.850 was amended to include Rule 3.850(b)(3) which provides an exception to the two-year period of limitations for filing a 3.850 motion if "the defendant retained counsel to timely file a 3.850 motion and counsel, through neglect, failed to file the motion."

The *Steele* Court provided that the procedure for obtaining a belated 3.850 in the above mentioned circumstances would be to file a Petition for Writ of Habeas Corpus with the trial court requesting said a belated appeal. Such a petition would be properly filed pursuant to Rule 3.850(b)(3). The trial court should then hold an evidentiary hearing to determine if the attorney agreed to file a 3.850 motion but failed to do so in a timely manner. If the habeas corpus petitioner should prevail at the hearing, he should be authorized to belatedly file a rule 3.850 motion challenging his conviction or sentence.

Just as attorneys can fail to timely file a 3.850 motion, attorneys sometimes fail to timely file a notice of appeal from the denial of a postconviction motion. If a notice of appeal is not timely filed for such a reason, it does not necessarily mean that the postconviction movant is forever barred from appealing the denial of a 3.850. In *Williams v. State*, 777 So.2d 947 (Fla.2000), the Florida Supreme Court extended the ruling in *Steele* to cases where postconviction counsel agreed to file a timely notice of appeal and failed to do so. In such a situation, the *Williams* Court held that a postconviction movant/appellant should be granted a belated appeal of the denial of the 3.850. Florida Rule of Appellate Procedure 9.141(c) provides for the filing of a habeas corpus petition, to the appellate court, requesting a belated appeal.

Finally, while *Steele* and *Williams* do apply to their specific fact situations, it is important to note that under the proper circumstances, the Florida Supreme Court saw fit to extend the protections against ineffective counsel to the postconviction context. Therefore, the rationales of *Steele* and *Williams* might be successfully argued in other postconviction contexts to extend that "more flexible standards of due process announced in the Fifth Amendment of the United States Constitution" depending on the facts of the case. I recommend that postconviction petitioners keep these cases in mind for their fact specific applications, and, if applicable, for other scenarios where the logic of said rulings may apply to other aspects of their cases. I hope that this article helps persons who have had attorneys who have dropped the ball on their postconviction cases. And, I recommend that persons who have not yet retained postconviction counsel retain a competent and experienced postconviction attorney to avoid the necessity of the above-discussed situations in the first place.

PUBLIC RECORDS REQUESTS

When one investigates his case for potential postconviction claims he typically refers to pretrial discovery documents, trial transcripts, the record on appeal, and correspondence from the trial attorney. All of these documents are valuable and, when properly reviewed, can present viable postconviction claims. But, an often of overlooked source of potential claims is the State Attorney's file. Said file is, for the most part, a public record and can be viewed by anyone who makes a request. The purpose of this article is to direct interested persons on how to obtain public records such as a prosecutor's file on a criminal case.

Article I, §24(a) of the Florida Constitution provides that:

> "every person has the right to inspect or copy any public record made or received in connection with the official business of any public body, officer or employee of the state . . . ."

In addition to the Florida Constitution, Florida Statutes §119, the *Public Records Act*, is the vehicle that affords the public access to most public information. §119.011 defines public records as " . . . all documents, papers, letters, maps, books, tapes, photographs, films, sound recordings, data processing software, or other material, regardless of the physical form, characteristics, or means of transmission, made or received pursuant to law or ordinance or in connection with the transaction of official business by any agency." In other words, public documents include all materials made or received by an agency in connection with official business that are used to perpetuate, communicate, or formalize knowledge. *See, Shevin v. Byron, et.al.,* 379 So. 640 (Fla. 1980). For the most part, any and all records received by a public agency are public records unless they are subject to an exception provided by Chapter 119. For the purposes of this article, important exceptions to be aware of are:

- *Active* criminal investigative and intelligence information.
- Attorney "work product" in an active case.
- Identity of crime victims in child abuse and sexual offense cases.
- Addresses and phone numbers of law enforcement officers and former officers and their families.

Other exemptions from Chapter 119 can be found in §119.071. But, for the most part, Chapter 119 is based upon the premise that all records of a public agency are public records unless excluded by a specific exemption. The public records law is to be construed liberally in favor of openness, and all exemptions from disclosure are to be construed narrowly and limited to their designated purpose. *See, City of St. Petersburg v. Romine ex rel. Dillinger,* 719 So.2d 19, 23 (Fla. 2nd DCA 1998).

For readers of this article it is important to know that a prosecutor's file on a case may be a public record that can be reviewed by any person who so requests. Of course, State Attorney case files on active cases will be considered to come under the *active criminal investigative* or *criminal intelligence* exemptions of Chapter 119. But, once a criminal case is disposed of and the disposition is final, the entire State Attorney's file on the case becomes a public record under Chapter 119. This means that the entire file (excluding any portions that are covered by a specific exemption) is open to viewing by anybody who makes a public records request.

Of course it is quite possible that a prosecutor's notes may come under the *work product* exemption. However, the work product exemption only provides for such an exemption "until the conclusion of the litigation or adversarial administrative proceedings." §119.071(d)(1). Therefore, if a case has already gone through trial and the direct appeal has concluded, the *work product* exemption arguably does not apply. *See, Tribune Co. v. Public Records*, 493 So.2d 480 (Fla. 2nd DCA 1986) [once criminal defendant's direct appeal became final, their investigative files are no longer considered active, despite the possibility of later postconviction proceedings]; and, *State v. Kokal*, 562 So.2d 324 (Fla. 1990).

One never knows what type of information may become available when reviewing the State Attorney's file. Be sure to be alert for information and or evidence that is noted in the files but which was never disclosed to you or your attorney. If any such nuggets should appear, they could potentially provide grounds for a 3.850 motion based upon newly discovered evidence, *Brady* violations, etc. While it is not possible to list every potential issue that could arise upon the viewing of the prosecutor's files, it is important to note that such a public records request may be very helpful in preparing a postconviction attack on a Judgment and Sentence.

If you are reading this article, it is most likely that you are incarcerated and will be unable to conduct a review of a prosecutor's files on your own. Therefore, I recommend, if possible, that an attorney experienced in such matters be retained to assist with the request and review of the prosecutor's files. In the alternative, a friend or family member could conduct the search on an incarcerated person's behalf. But, it will be important for the reviewer to be extremely familiar with the facts of the case being reviewed so as to know when something interesting/helpful appears in the prosecutor's file.

Chapter 119 provides that: "Every person who has custody of a public record shall permit the record to be inspected and examined by any person desiring to do so, at any reasonable time, under reasonable conditions, and under supervision by the custodian of the public record or the custodian's designee." The custodian shall furnish a copy or a certified copy of the record upon payment of the fee prescribed by law, and for all other copies, upon payment of the actual cost of duplication of the record. §119.07(4) provides more information on the costs of copies and duplication of records. Be aware that one may incur costs when performing a public records review.

To make a public records request all one must do is contact the records custodian for the public agency and ask to view specific records. The request does not even have to be in writing. Nevertheless, it is always beneficial to put the request in writing and request that the custodian specify, in writing, any §119 exemptions it is claiming. It will behoove the public records requestor to make a paper trail in case he needs to bring a civil action to enforce public records viewing rights. Therefore, it is best to make a *specific* written request for the records one wishes to see. Once the request is made, the records custodian must be given a reasonable time to retrieve the records and delete any portions that the custodian claims are exempt. Said "reasonable time" is the only delay that is permitted for producing the public records for inspection. *The Tribune Company v. Cannella*, 458 So.2d 1075 (Fla. 1984).

Once a public records request is made, the custodian must permit the inspection at any reasonable time, under reasonable conditions, and under supervision by the custodian of the public record or the custodian's designee. *See* §119.07(1)(a). The custodian cannot refuse to produce the requested records just because some parts of the record are exempted. Instead, the custodian shall delete or excise the exempted portions and produce the nonexempted record portions. *See* §119.07)(1)(d). Once again, when making public records requests, it is wise to be aware that the custodian can charge for copies and for extensive use of technology and clerical or supervisory costs. §119.07(4)(d).

If, for some reason, the custodian fails to act on a public records request, the proper remedy is a petition for a writ of mandamus in the appropriate circuit court. *Staton v. McMillan*, 597 So.2d 940 (Fla. 1st DCA 1992). Such a petition should seek to compel the custodian of the records to comply with the public records request. But, before filing a mandamus petition the petitioner must first furnish a public records request to the agency involved. It will help to attach your written public records request as an exhibit to the petition. It is also important to note that if a mandamus petitioner succeeds in obtaining the records via a civil action (mandamus petition) §119.12 provides for attorneys fees. §119.12 specifically provides that "[i]f a civil action is filed against an agency to enforce the provisions of this chapter and if the court determines that such agency unlawfully refused to permit a public record to be inspected, examined, or copied, the court shall assess and award, against the agency responsible, the reasonable costs of enforcement including reasonable attorneys' fees."

A public records search of the prosecutor's file may not always turn up information helpful to a postconviction case. On the other hand, one never knows, the file could be rife with newly discovered evidence claims. Therefore, it is important to consider conducting such a public records search to discover, support or supplement a postconviction claim.

SPLIT SENTENCES
and VIOLATIONS of PROBATION

Oftentimes when a criminal defendant on a probationary portion of a split sentence (for purposes of this article a split sentence is a prison sentence followed by a term of probation) admits to a violation of probation and agrees to a new prison sentence, the advice given by counsel is incomplete as it pertains to previously earned gain-time. Many trial lawyers are not familiar with DOC's treatment of previously earned gain-time and thus misadvise their clients as to how the previously earned gain-time will affect the new sentence. I have represented numerous inmates who were informed by their attorneys that they would receive credit for all previously earned gain-time against their new sentence. Unfortunately, trial attorneys are often unfamiliar with Florida Statute §944.28(1), which provides DOC with the authority to forfeit previously earned gain-time upon a violation of a probationary portion of a split sentence.

Florida Statutes §948.28(1) provides that if probation is revoked for a defendant who already served a term of incarceration under a split sentence, DOC " . . . may, without notice or hearing, declare a forfeiture of all gain-time earned according to the provisions of law by such prisoner prior to . . . his or her release under such clemency, conditional release, probation, community control, provisional release, control release, or parole." §948.28(1) effectively allows DOC to forfeit the previously earned gain-time and forces the defendant to serve the forfeited time before the newly negotiated sentence can begin. In other words, if a defendant enters an admission to a violation of probation pursuant to a plea deal for a specific prison sentence, DOC will make the person serve the remainder (forfeited gain-time) of the original prison sentence before the new sentence can commence. Therefore, §948.28(1) allows DOC to thwart the intention of the negotiated plea by adding more time onto the negotiated sentence.

If a defendant is not properly advised as to the effect of §948.28(1) on a plea to a violation of a probationary portion of a split sentence and his previously earned gain-time is forfeited, then the plea is rendered involuntary and is subject to being withdrawn. A plea of guilty is constitutionally valid only to the extent that it is voluntary and intelligent. *Brady v. United States*, 397 U.S. 742 (1970). Three requirements are essential for a valid guilty plea: (1) the plea must be voluntary; (2) the defendant must understand the nature of the charge and the consequences of his plea; and, (3) there must be a factual basis for the plea. *Williams v. State*, 316 So.2d 267 (Fla. 1975). If a defendant does not understand that additional time (the forfeited gain-time) will be added back onto the newly imposed sentence (thereby increasing the negotiated sentence) then said defendant clearly does not have a clear understanding as to the consequences of his plea. Such a plea would, thus, be rendered involuntary if in fact DOC forfeited the previously earned gain-time and forced the defendant to serve a longer sentence than was actually negotiated.

Florida case law specifically provides relief for the above situation. In *McAllister v. State*, 821 So.2d 1250 (Fla. 1st DCA 2002), the defendant entered into a plea agreement to receive ten years credit for time served on a seventeen year sentence following the revocation of probation and was sentenced in accordance with the agreement. DOC revoked the gain-time portion of the original ten years in accordance with Florida Statutes §948.28(1). The defendant in *McAllister* claimed in a 3.850 motion that he entered into the plea agreement with the understanding that he would receive credit for the full ten years. McAllister asked that the trial court either: (1) resentence him in a manner that would enforce his plea agreement; or, (2) allow him to withdraw his plea. The *McAllister* Court stated:

"While the trial court cannot compel the DOC to follow the plea agreement, since it would usurp the DOC's authority to forfeit gain time, the trial court can still effectuate the plea agreement by either resentencing the appellant in a manner that will effectuate the plea agreement given the DOC's forfeiture, or by allowing the appellant to withdraw from his plea." *Id.*

Therefore, if a defendant is to be resentenced, he should be resentenced so that he would serve the amount of time he actually pleaded to, instead of said amount of time plus the forfeited gain-time. The *McAllister* Court further explained that "effectuating the plea agreement is proper even though the appellant had no legal entitlement to such gain-time since the DOC could declare it forfeited, because the court and the parties contemplated that the appellant would be credited with such gain-time." *Id.*

McAllister, a First District Court of Appeal case, is in accord with the other district courts of appeal in Florida. See, *Foldi v. State*, 695 So.2d 886 (Fla. 2nd DCA 1997); *Williams v. Department of Corrections*, 734 So.2d 1132 (Fla. 3rd DCA 1999); and, *Dellahoy v. State*, 816 So.2d 1253 (Fla. 5th DCA 2002). Therefore, should DOC forfeit gain-time from a previously served sentence upon the violation of probation, there is a remedy if there was a negotiated plea agreement which did not take the effect of Florida Statutes §948.28(1) into account. The sentence should be restructured to reflect the intent of the parties or the plea should be allowed to be withdrawn.

INVOLUNTARY PLEA DUE to MISADVICE of COUNSEL

When one facing criminal charges is making a decision about going to trial, an important consideration is whether any type of plea offer has been extended by the prosecution. Sometimes defense attorneys do not effectively represent their clients in this aspect of the representation. A plea may not have been relayed to a client because the attorney assumed the client would not accept the offer. Other times the attorney may relay the plea but either not inform, or misinform, his client about crucial aspects of said plea. In either case, such a defendant does have recourse via a Rule 3.850 motion. A guilty plea is not voluntary or intelligent if advice given by defense counsel, and on which a defendant relies in entering a plea, falls below a level of reasonable competence such that the defendant does not receive effective assistance of counsel. *U.S. v. Loughery*, 908 F.2d 1014 (D.C. Cir. 1990).

To effectively represent a client in a criminal matter, an attorney has the duty to adequately counsel his client as to the advisability of accepting or rejecting a plea offer from the State. Failure to fully advise a client of the ramifications of accepting or rejecting a plea offer can constitute ineffective assistance of counsel. *See, Young v. State*, 625 So.2d 906 (Fla. 2d DCA, 1993); *Wilson v. State*, 647 So.2d 185 (Fla. 1st DCA, 1994). Courts appear uniformly to hold that the failure of trial counsel to communicate or to communicate correctly the facts and merits of a plea bargain offered by the State may warrant postconviction relief for a criminal defendant. *Young v.*

State, 608 So.2d 111 (Fla. 5th DCA, 1992).

The misadvice of an attorney, in the plea context, as to how long the defendant will have to actually serve on a sentence can constitute ineffective assistance of counsel. *Garmon v. Lockhart*, 938 F.2d 120 (8th Cir. 1991). A defendant's guilty plea is considered involuntary if it is induced by a defense counsel's promise which is not kept, and a defendant may withdraw his plea if he was misled and induced to plead by his counsel's mistaken advice. *Ricardo v. State*, 647 So.2d 287 (Fla. 2nd DCA 1994).

Whether or not defense counsel believes his client will accept any given plea offer, said counsel still has a duty to inform his client of any plea offers. *See* Fla. R.Crim. P. 3.171(c)(2). Counsel's misadvice, or lack of advice, in regards to acceptance of a plea offer can constitute ineffective assistance of counsel. *Boria v. Keane*, 99 F.3d 492 (2d Cir. 1996). And, the failure to timely relay a plea offer to a client can constitute ineffective assistance of counsel. See *Cottle v. State*, 733 so.2d 963 (1999). In order to prove that an attorney was ineffective for failing to convey a plea offer to a client, the following must be shown: (1) counsel failed to communicate a plea offer; (2) the defendant would have accepted the plea offer had he been properly advised; and, (3) that the acceptance of the plea offer would have resulted in a lesser sentence. *Id.*

In *Garcia v. State*, 736 So.2d 89 (Fla. 4th DCA 1999), the Fourth District Court of Appeal for Florida dealt specifically with the issue of ineffective assistance of counsel for failure to properly relay a plea offer. Francisco Garcia was charged with shooting into an occupied dwelling and second-degree murder. *Id.* Subsequent to his conviction, Mr. Garcia filed a 3.850 which alleged that his attorney failed to properly inform him of the consequences of pleading guilty and, thereby, improperly induced Garcia not to accept the State's plea offer. *Id.* The trial court summarily denied Garcia's 3.850. *Id.*

Prior to trial the State made an offer to Garcia whereby Mr. Garcia would receive a sentence of five and one half years in exchange for a guilty plea. *Id.* Garcia acknowledged that his attorney did relay the plea offer to him, but, only at the last minute. *Id.* Garcia further alleged that his attorney:

failed to discuss with Garcia the details and the strength of the State's case; urged Garcia not to take the deal because he would succeed at trial; erroneously advised Garcia that he would get one-third knocked off of any sentence he did receive; and, failed to advise Garcia that he was subject to a three-year minimum mandatory for the use of a firearm. *Id.* Garcia further alleged in his 3.850 that had he been properly advised by his attorney, he would have taken the plea deal offered by the State prior to trial, and, that he would have served far less time in prison. *Id.*

On appeal of the summary denial of his 3.850, the Fourth DCA held that Garcia did present a facially sufficient claim for ineffectiveness of counsel for failure to relay a plea offer. *Id.* at 90. The *Garcia* Court further noted that in *Cottle v. State*, 733 so.2d 963 (1999), the Florida Supreme Court did not provide what the appropriate remedy would be where counsel failed to timely relay a plea offer to a client. The *Garcia* Court decided that if a defendant does establish ineffectiveness of counsel for failure to relay a plea offer, it should be left to the trial court to "fashion a remedy that 'is tailored to the injury suffered and [does] not unnecessarily infringe on competing interests.'" *Id.* at 90, *quoting United States v. Morrison*, 449 U.S. 361 (1981).

Therefore, some sort of relief may be due if a plea was not relayed by defense counsel or if counsel failed to properly explain the plea. In either case, it may be possible to obtain a better result via a Rule 3.850 Motion. If the plea was never relayed, it may be possible to obtain the original plea offer if it can be demonstrated that counsel failed to relay the plea and the defendant would have accepted said plea. Such a result might be obtained by seeking relief under *Garcia*, whereby the trial court would fashion a remedy tailored to the injury suffered, i.e., the denial of the ability to accept the original plea. If the benefit of the original plea offer cannot be obtained, it may still be possible to withdraw the plea entirely and return to a pretrial posture.

Of course, as with any postconviction venture, I would advise anybody looking into such a course of action to seriously consider if he will be better off with a withdrawal of the plea. Often pleas are given in exchange for a reduced sentence or a waiver of the State's right to pursue sentence enhancements (such as habitual offender, prison releasee reoffender, or minimum mandatory sentences). Therefore, before any attempt to withdraw a plea is made, I strongly advise any such person to consider if they will actually be better off if they do pursue a withdrawal of the plea. If the dangers of withdrawal of the plea are not great, or if you are willing to gamble with your potential sentence, then it may be advisable to pursue a withdrawal of the plea. But, such a decision should only be made after fully investigating the potential sentence that you are subject to upon withdrawal of the plea.

WRIT of MANDAMUS

Once a motion for postconviction relief is filed with a trial court, the movant can typically count on a lengthy wait before he will hear anything back from the court. While some of the circuit courts have postconviction divisions and move their cases along at a reasonable speed, it is more often the case that a postconviction motion will progress through the court system at a snail's pace. Unfortunately, the courts do not have speedy trial concerns on postconviction cases. As a result, such cases are often put on the back burner by the courts while more pressing matters are addressed in other cases.

It is not unusual for a postconviction motion to languish for over a year before the trial court even issues an order to show cause to the State. Unfortunately, due to the low priority often given to such motions by the courts, this is common. If a court takes too long to issue any rulings on a postconviction motion, the movant does have recourse. Florida Rule of Judicial Administration 2.215(f) provides that, "Every judge has a duty to rule upon and announce an order or judgment on every matter submitted to that judge within a reasonable time." While the *reasonable time* standard is somewhat vague, it does still place the burden on the court to deal with any motions presented.

If a trial judge fails to rule on a motion within a reasonable time, a petition for writ of mandamus is the proper remedy. *Mason v. Circuit Court*, 603 So.2d 94 (Fla. 5th DCA 1992); *Matthews v. Circuit Court*, 515 So.2d 1065 (Fla. 5th

DCA 1987); See also *Berens v. Cobb*, 539 So.2d 24 (Fla. 2nd DCA 1989) [mandamus was proper remedy where judge refused to rule on a motion]. A trial court has a legal duty to rule on a postconviction motion. In the absence of a timely ruling on a postconviction motion, the trial court can be compelled, via a writ of mandamus from the appellate court, to issue a ruling on the motion. *Matthews v. Circuit Court*, 515 So.2d 1065 (Fla. 5th DCA 1987).

As with any motion or petition, it is wise to evaluate whether the petition for a writ of mandamus should be filed. As a general rule of thumb, it is safe to say that one should wait at least six months before attempting to compel the trial court to rule on a postconviction motion via a mandamus petition. Thereafter, if the court has not dealt with the postconviction motion, it may be time to pursue mandamus to obtain a ruling on the motion.

Prior to filing for a writ of mandamus, the movant should first request action from the trial court. A brief motion requesting that the trial court rule on the postconviction motion should suffice. It is wise to note in such a motion how long the postconviction motion has been pending. Such a motion may, in and of itself, spur the trial court into action. If the trial court still refuses to rule on the postconviction motion, then it may be time to file for mandamus with the appellate court.

If the postconviction motion is filed with a circuit court (as will most likely be the case), then the Petition for Writ of Mandamus should be filed with the applicable appellate court pursuant to Florida Rule of Appellate Procedure 9.100. The nature of the relief sought in the petition should be to compel the trial court to rule on the pending postconviction motion. The following should be noted in the petition:

(1) The name of the court to which the writ of mandamus should be issued;

(2) The trial court case number;

(3) The date that the postconviction motion was filed with the trial court;

(4) The fact that action on the postconviction motion has already been requested; and,

(5) The fact that the trial court has not issued any ruling on the postconviction motion.

Often the mere act of filing a mandamus petition with the district court will prompt the trial court to take action on a postconviction motion. If the trial court does not issue a ruling after the mandamus petition is filed, it is likely that the district court will direct the trial court to explain the lack of action on the case. If there is not a reasonable explanation for the delay, the district court will likely issue a writ of mandamus directing the lower court to rule on the postconviction motion.

Mandamus can be a useful tool for obtaining a ruling from a trial court. Nevertheless, I recommend that it be used sparingly. One must always keep in mind that filing a petition for writ of mandamus with the higher court may offend the trial court. And, if the writ of mandamus is issued, the case will be going right back before the judge who has been ordered to take action. Therefore, I recommend that anybody who is considering pursuing mandamus relief weigh their need for a prompt ruling against the possibility of offending the trial court and, thus, making it more difficult to convince the trial court to grant relief. Each case is different. Sometimes it is worth it to pursue mandamus relief. Sometimes it is better to wait and let the case work itself through the system. As was noted, a mandamus petition should probably not be filed until the postconviction motion has been pending for at least six months. Additionally, I would recommend, in most cases, that mandamus relief not be pursued until the case has been pending for at least one year with no action from the court. This is especially so for inmates with lengthy sentences. Sometimes it is just better to let the court take its time without being pressured to rule. Nevertheless, mandamus is always an option to be considered and can be helpful in some cases.

THE RULE of LENITY

Oftentimes when a criminal offense is charged, the specific date of the offense can be pinpointed. In such a circumstance, it is easy to determine which set of sentencing guidelines will apply to the offense. However, sometimes the offense is alleged to have occurred within a period of time which spans several sets of sentencing guidelines. When it is charged that a criminal offense occurred over a period of time during which sentencing laws have changed, the defendant should be sentenced under the more lenient version of the sentencing laws. *Cairl v. State*, 833 So.2d 312 (Fla. 2nd DCA 2003). Sometimes in such a situation, though, the court and defense counsel fail to recognize which set of guidelines should actually apply. If an attorney fails to have his client sentenced under the proper set of guidelines in the above scenario, then the attorney's representation is ineffective, the sentence should be vacated, and a new sentence should be imposed under the proper, more lenient guidelines. See, *Torres v. State*, 879 So.2d 1254 (Fla. 3rd DCA 2004).

In *Cairl v. State*, 833 So.2d 312 (Fla. 2nd DCA 2003), the defendant was convicted of several sexual offenses relating to a person under the age of sixteen. The trial court originally sentenced Cairl under the 1995 sentencing guidelines. Cairl was resentenced under the 1994 sentencing guidelines pursuant to *Heggs v. State*, 759 So.2d 620 (Fla. 2000). However, the trial court denied Cairl's claim that he should be sentenced under the most lenient guidelines in effect during the time frame alleged in the information, and, instead, applied the sentencing guidelines in effect on the end date alleged in the information. *Cairl* at 312.

Cairl was charged with two single offenses alleged to have occurred on or between January 1, 1991, and February 4, 1997. *Id.* Cairl argued that because the dates straddled three different sentencing guideline time frames and because neither the evidence nor the verdict pinpointed the date of the offenses, he was entitled to be sentenced under the most lenient version of the three sentencing guidelines. Said most lenient version was the one in effect between January 1, 1991, and April 7, 1992. *Id.* The Second District Court of Appeal of Florida agreed with Cairl's argument and remanded his case for resentencing under the least harsh sentencing guidelines. The *Cairl* Court did so based upon the Rule of Lenity. *Id.* at 314. It was held, pursuant to the Rule of Lenity, that when the sentencing laws change during a period in which a defendant is alleged to have committed an offense, the defendant should be sentenced under the more lenient version of the guidelines. *Id.*; See also *Schloesser v. State*, 697 So.2d 942 (Fla. 2nd DCA 1997); *Duer v. Moore*, 765 So.2d 743 (Fla. 1st DCA); *Maitre v. State*, 770 So.2d 309 (Fla. 4th DCA 2000); and *Gilbert v. State*, 680 So.2nd 1132 (Fla. 3rd DCA 1996).

A sentencing issue based upon the Rule of Lenity should be preserved by trial counsel at the time of sentencing and raised on direct appeal. However, attorneys sometimes neglect of forget to raise the issue either at the trial court level or on appeal. In such a circumstance, the improper sentencing can either be raised in a Florida Rule of Criminal Procedure 3.850 Motion for Postconviction Relief or a petition for writ of habeas corpus alleging ineffectiveness of appellate counsel. The failure to ensure proper sentencing under the most lenient guidelines will have to be addressed as an issue of ineffectiveness of counsel. Or, the improper sentencing can also be addressed in a Florida Rule of Criminal Procedure 3.800 Motion to Correct Sentence pursuant to Rule 3.800(a).

In order to address the ineffectiveness of counsel issue it will have to be demonstrated that: (1) counsel performed deficiently; and, (2) the performance actually prejudiced the defendant. *Strickland v. Washington*, 466 U.S. 668 (1984). Clearly an attorney's failure to ensure that his client is sentenced under more lenient sentencing guidelines falls below an objective standard of reasonableness and is thus ineffective. Additionally, if it is clear that the sentence that a defendant would have received (in the absence of his attorney's ineffectiveness) would be less than that received under the improper, and harsher, guidelines, then the prejudice prong of *Strickland* is also apparent.

As mentioned above, an ineffectiveness of counsel/Rule of Lenity claim should either be addressed in a Rule 3.850 Motion for Postconviction Relief or in a petition for a writ of habeas corpus (filed with the appellate court) alleging ineffectiveness of appellate counsel. Depending on the circumstances it may be wise to pursue both collateral attacks on the sentence. Whichever procedural vehicle is chosen (3.850 or habeas petition), it will be subject to a two-year period of limitations.

If a defendant is outside of the two-year period of limitations for the 3.850 and habeas corpus petition, there is still the possibility of addressing the issue in a Florida Rule of Criminal Procedure 3.800(a) Motion to Correct Sentence. Rule 3.800(a) provides that "[a] court may at any time correct an illegal sentence imposed by it in a sentencing scoresheet . . . " *See Sheely v. State*, 820 So.2d 1080 (Fla. 2nd DCA 2002) [a sentence that is entered pursuant to guidelines which have not been constitutionally enacted is an illegal sentence and is subject to correction pursuant to Rule 3.800(a)]; and, *Carpenter v. State*, 870 So. 2d 955 (Fla. 1st DCA 2004) [defendant raised facially sufficient claim for relief that his sentence was in excess of statutory maximum, where trial court record contained sentencing guidelines from incorrect year which did not reflect year in which defendant committed offense, and thus, postconviction court was required to grant relief or attach portions of record conclusively refuting claim of illegal sentence].

Thus, there are a number of ways in which one can raise a Rule of Lenity issue after the Judgment and Sentence has become final. Each case is different and one procedural vehicle may be more appropriate than another depending on the circumstances. One will need to consider the specific facts of his case to determine which of the above-addressed collateral attacks would be most appropriate for his sentence. But, if a sentence has been improperly applied due to a violation of the Rule of Lenity, the problem possibly can be corrected and a reduced sentence may result.

IMPROPER FLAT FEE ARRANGEMENTS and ATTORNEY CONFLICT OF INTERESTS

A common fee arrangement with an attorney for a criminal case consists of a one-time payment of a flat-fee, for which the attorney will perform all services necessary, up to and including a trial. The flat-fee arrangement is usually a fair contract which will serve to ensure that a criminal defendant receives sufficient representation while at the same time imposing a cap on the amount that is spent on the case. Sometimes, though, if the fee agreement is not properly structured, it can work to the disadvantage of the client. Some attorneys' fee arrangements provide for a flat-fee payment which will cover the attorney fees as well as any expenses which are incurred in conducting the defense. This type of agreement creates a serious conflict of interests which could work to the detriment of the client's case. Inherent in such an arrangement is the temptation for the attorney to cut corners on the preparation of the defense in order to limit the amount of the flat fee which will be spent on investigation of the case, deposition costs, expert witness fees, etc. In other words, the less money that is spent on client expenses means more money which goes toward the attorney's fee.

A flat fee retainer arrangement which also encompasses client expenses is an actual conflict of interests which may present a viable postconviction issue for a collateral attack on a judgment and sentence. Implicit in the Sixth Amendment of the United States' Constitution's guarantee of the right to counsel is the right to the effective assistance of counsel. An actual conflict of interest on the part of trial counsel can impair the performance of a lawyer and ultimately result in a finding that the defendant did not receive effective assistance of counsel. *Lee v. State*, 690 So.2d 664 (Fla. 1st DCA 1997); *Cuyler v. Sullivan*, 446 U.S. 335 (1980). To prove an ineffectiveness claim premised on an alleged conflict of interest the defendant must establish both: (1) that his attorney had an actual conflict of interest; and, (2) that said conflict affected the lawyer's performance. *Herring v. State*, 730 So.2d 1264 (Fla. 1998).

If the issue of counsel's actual conflict is preserved and raised on direct appeal, the failure of a trial court to conduct an inquiry and appoint separate counsel requires that the resulting conviction automatically be reversed. *Lee v. State*, 690 So.2d 664 (Fla. 1st DCA 1997); *Holloway v. Arkansas*, 435 U.S. 475 (1978). A different rule is applied, however, if the issue of an attorney's conflict of interests is raised in a postconviction proceeding. When ineffective assistance of counsel is first asserted in a postconviction motion, the defendant must show that the conflict impaired the performance of the defense lawyer. *Cuyler v. Sullivan*, 446 U.S. at 348. Even then, though, "it is not necessary to show that counsel's deficient performance resulting from the conflict affected the outcome of the trial. As the Court held in *Sullivan*, prejudice is presumed." *Lee v. State*, 690 So.2d at 669 (Fla. 1st DCA 1997).

Therefore, if an improper fee arrangement (or any other situation which creates an "actual" conflict of interests) was present, there may be an available postconviction attack on the judgment and sentence. If such an issue is available, it should be raised in a Florida Rule of Criminal Procedure 3.850 Motion for Postconviction Relief. It is important to point out both: (1) that an actual conflict of interests existed; and, (2) that the conflict of interests impaired the performance of the defense attorney. If issues of failure to properly prepare a case, investigate a case, or other like deficiencies exist, these issues should be argued to show that the attorney's performance was adversely affected by the conflict of interests. It is important to understand that even though the conflict of interests creates a presumption of prejudice, said presumption is not irrefutable. Obviously, the conflict issue becomes stronger with more facts demonstrating prejudice to the defendant. Therefore, it is important to argue any facts which demonstrate how the attorney failed the client as a result of the conflict.

ACTUAL INNOCENCE CLAIMS

A State inmate seeking to attack his Judgment and Sentence in the federal courts can do so by filing a Title 28 of the United States Code (U.S.C.) §2254 federal petition for writ of habeas corpus. However, there are numerous requirements before the merits of a §2254 petition will even be considered by the federal courts. Firstly, as with 3.850 motions, there is a period of limitations which can serve to bar consideration of a 2254 petition. Title 28 U.S.C. §2244(d)(1) provides a one-year period of limitation for filing the federal petition. However, should a case appear to be outside of the one-year period of limitations, the postconviction litigator may still be able to obtain a review of the constitutional claims if a showing of *actual innocence* can be made.

Pursuant to Title 28 U.S.C. §2244(d)(1) the one-year period of limitation shall begin running from the latest of the following:

(1) The date on which the judgment became final by the conclusion of direct review or the expiration of the time for seeking such review;

(2) The date on which the impediment to filing an application created by State action, in violation of the Constitution or laws of the United States, is removed, if the applicant was prevented from filing by such State action;

(3) The date on which the constitutional right asserted was

initially recognized by the United States Supreme Court, if
the right has been newly recognized by the Supreme Court
and made retroactively applicable to cases on collateral
review; or,

(4) The date on which the factual predicate of the claim or claims
could have been discovered through the exercise of due
diligence.

If a case appears to be outside of the one-year period of limitations
imposed by §2244(d), the postconviction movant may still be able to seek
review of the constitutional claims. Exceptions to procedural rules have been
made in situations where it would be equitable to do so. Habeas corpus is, in
essence, an equitable remedy. *Schlup v. Delo*, 513 U.S. 298 (1995). The U.S.
Supreme Court has consistently recognized exceptions to the procedural
rules when it is necessary to prevent a miscarriage of justice. "The individual
interest in avoiding injustice is most compelling in the context of actual
innocence." *Schlup* at 325. It has been held that a petitioner's *actual
innocence* may provide a "gateway" to allow federal constitutional claims to
be heard in a §2254 proceeding in situations where the petitioner is otherwise
procedurally barred by the applicable period of limitations.

In *Schlup*, it was held that although a federal habeas petitioner's *actual
innocence* is not itself a constitutional claim on which relief can be based, it is
considered a "gateway" which allows a petitioner to have otherwise
procedurally barred claims considered on their merits. *Id.* at 315. In other
words, a claim of innocence "does not by itself provide a basis for relief." *Id.* at
315. The *actual innocence* claim is a procedural claim which is offered to
demonstrate that the petitioner's case is one of a select category of cases which
implicate "a fundamental miscarriage of justice" and, thus, allow the court to
consider the merits of the procedurally defaulted claim. *Id.* If actual
innocence is demonstrated, then the procedurally barred claims of
constitutional deprivations (such as ineffective assistance of counsel claims)
can be considered on their merits. As provided in *Schlup*, a claim of *actual
innocence* is "not itself a constitutional claim, but instead a gateway through

which a habeas petitioner must pass to have his otherwise barred constitutional claim considered on the merits."

In making an *actual innocence* claim, the burden is on the petitioner to present new evidence (not presented at trial) which demonstrates that it is more likely than not that no reasonable juror would have convicted him in light of the new evidence. The standard provided in *Schlup* is that "in light of the new evidence, no juror, acting reasonably, would have voted to find [the petitioner] guilty beyond a reasonable doubt." *Id.* at 329. This is indeed a heavy burden on the habeas petitioner seeking to avoid a procedural bar.

Actual Innocence, for the purposes of this article means factual, as opposed to legal, innocence. By alleging *actual innocence*, the claim would have to be that the movant actually did not commit the crime. *McCleskey v. Zant*, 499 U.S. 467 (1991). The term actual innocence essentially means that in light of the new evidence, a reasonable trier of fact could not find all of the elements necessary to convict the defendant of the particular crime. Furthermore, *actual innocence* has been defined as meaning that the conviction was of a person who was innocent of the specific crime for which he was charged and convicted, not that the petitioner was not present at the scene of the offense. *Johnson v. Hargett*, 978 F.2d 855 (5th Cir. 1992).

The petitioner must support the claim of actual innocence with new and reliable evidence which was not presented at trial. *Schlup* at 324. In reviewing an *actual innocence claim*, the presiding court must "consider all relevant evidence: that [was] presented at trial; that [was] arguably wrongly excluded from trial; and that [was] unavailable at trial." *Battle v. Delo*, 64 F.3d 347, 352 (8th Cir. 1985). And, such an evaluation must be reviewed with an understanding that "proof beyond a reasonable doubt marks the legal boundary between guilt and innocence." *Schlup* at 328. Should the petitioner be able to make the necessary showing, his constitutional claims should be considered by the reviewing court, even though they would otherwise be procedurally barred. The *actual innocence* exception to the one-year period of limitations sets a high standard to get past the procedural bar. But, if such an argument is available, it may be a feasible way of obtaining review of otherwise procedurally barred claims.

ATTORNEY/CLIENT PHONE CALLS

As an attorney who represents only inmates, I have found again and again that it is a fight to be able to have confidential telephone contact with my clients. Fortunately, my office is experienced in dealing with the Department of Corrections and we always make sure that our telephone calls are attorney/client privileged calls that are conducted on a secured, unmonitored line. Unfortunately, though, it seems that many attorneys do not insist on private phone calls with their incarcerated clients. This can be problematic for several reasons. A prisoner who has to speak on the phone while a DOC employee is sitting in the same room is not going to feel comfortable in candidly discussing his interests with his attorney. Furthermore, if legal matters are discussed in the presence of a third party, said discussion serves to waive the attorney client privilege for any such matters discussed. *U.S. v. Blackburn*, 446 F.2d 1089 (C.A.Fla. 1971) [where third persons were present at time communications between defendant and attorney were made, communications were not privileged]. As such, it is imperative that inmates, and their attorneys, know their rights as far as attorney/client phone calls are concerned.

Florida Administrative Code, Chapter 33-602(3)(a) provides that, "Inmates shall be allowed to make private telephone calls to attorneys upon presentation to the warden or his designee of evidence that the call is necessary. Such evidence shall be a letter from the attorney (transmission by

FAX is acceptable) requesting the return call or a court order containing a deadline the inmate cannot meet if he must communicate by letter with the attorney." Chapter 33-602(3)(a) further provides that "An attorney shall also be permitted to make prior arrangements by letter or FAX with the warden or warden's designee to have the inmate client receive a private telephone call from the attorney on an unmonitored telephone." Such telephone calls to attorneys "shall not be monitored or electronically recorded. These calls will be placed on telephones designated for this purpose and shall be collect calls." Each institution is required to have at least one telephone that is not connected to the monitoring system for these calls.

Chapter 33-602(3)(a) is very specific as to the rights inmates have. Classification officers will often tell attorneys that the phone call has to be made from the officer's office and, further, that the officer refuses to leave an inmate alone in his office. Classification officers will often say that there is no such phone for private, unmonitored attorney/client calls. This is all untrue. Have your attorney insist on a private, unmonitored call, as is required by Chapter 33. If the classification officer is unwilling to comply with his duties, have your attorney contact the classification supervisor or even the warden of the institution. This usually will help to obtain the necessary private phone call.

Your communication with your attorney should be protected by the attorney/client privilege. When communicating with your attorney over the telephone, have the attorney insist on the private, unmonitored phone line. Do not allow the laziness of a classification officer to deprive you of the very important right.

NEWLY DISCOVERED
EVIDENCE CLAIMS

Florida Rule of Criminal Procedure 3.850 generally imposes a two-year period of limitations for filing a motion to collaterally attack a judgment and/or sentence. Rule 3.850 provides three exceptions to the two-year period of limitations: (1) *newly discovered evidence* — the facts on which the claim is predicated were unknown to the movant or the movant's attorney and could not have been ascertained by the exercise of due diligence; (2) *new rule of law* — the fundamental constitutional right asserted was not established within the two-year period of limitations and has been held to apply retroactively; or, (3) *ineffectiveness of postconviction counsel* — the defendant retained counsel to timely file a 3.850 motion and counsel, through neglect, failed to file the motion. This article will address the issue of newly discovered evidence and how to raise such an issue in a 3.850 motion.

In order to be considered newly discovered evidence for the purpose of setting aside a conviction, after trial, the evidence must have been unknown by the trial court and by the defendant or his counsel at time of trial. *Jones v. State*, 709 So.2d 512 (Fla. 1998). Furthermore, it must appear that the defendant and his counsel could not have known of the evidence by use of due diligence. *Id*. Finally, the evidence must be of such nature that it would probably produce acquittal on retrial. *Id*.

In the context of a guilty or nolo contendere plea, though, the standard for withdrawal of a plea due to newly discovered evidence is slightly different. The first two elements of *Jones* still must be proven (i.e., the evidence is newly discovered *and* it could not have been discovered through the exercise of due diligence). But, in the plea context a movant must prove that the withdrawal of the plea is necessary to correct a manifest injustice. *Bradford v. State*, 869 So.2d 28 (Fla. 2nd DCA 2004); *Scott v. State*, 629 So.2d 888 (Fla. 4th DCA 1993). Said standard is more appropriate for a case where there is a plea since *Jones* is "virtually impossible to apply because there was no trial and no evidence produced. Any determinations as to the nature and admissibility of the evidence would be speculative." *Bradford* at 29.

Newly discovered evidence issues which may garner postconviction relief include, but are not limited to:

- ◆ Eyewitness testimony which is exculpatory and could not have been discovered through the use of due diligence at the time of trial. *Clugston v. State*, 765 So.2d 816 (Fla. 4th DCA, 2000).

- ◆ A key State witness has recanted his or her testimony. *Stephens v. State*, 829 So.2d 945 (Fla. 1st DCA, 2002).

- ◆ The State suppressed exculpatory evidence or matters which could be used to impeach prosecution witnesses. *Taylor v. State*, 848 So.2d 410 (Fla. 1st DCA 2003).

- ◆ A codefendant received a life sentence after the defendant received a death sentence for the same offense. *Scott v. Dugger*, 604 So.2d 465 (Fla. 1992) ["[I]n a death case involving equally culpable codefendants the death sentence of one codefendant is subject to collateral review under rule 3.850 when another codefendant subsequently receives a life sentence."].

- ◆ A codefendant admits to refusing to testify on defendant's behalf and refusing to give exculpatory testimony for defendant because of coercion from the State. *Roundtree v. State*, 884 So.2d 322 (Fla. 2d DCA 2004).

Whether the conviction being attacked is the result of a jury trial or a guilty/*nolo contendere* plea, the burden on the postconviction movant is substantial. Firstly, the "new evidence" must be something that truly could not have been discovered through the use of due diligence at the time of the original proceedings. Therefore, if something could have easily been discovered by the movant and/or his counsel at the time of the trial/plea, the due diligence requirement will preclude the movant from raising the issue as newly discovered evidence. If anything, such a situation would more properly be raised as an ineffectiveness of counsel claim and, thus, be subject to the two-year period of limitations imposed by Rule 3.850.

Additionally, it must be shown the newly discovered evidence would have had a substantial impact on the likely outcome of the case. In the trial context, the movant must show that the new evidence would probably cause an acquittal at a new trial. This is a weighty burden which requires evidence that would strongly refute at least one of the elements of the offense charged at trial. Speculative evidence or witnesses with dubious credibility likely will not sustain the burden.

In the plea context, it is important to keep in mind that withdrawal of a *nolo contendere* plea, after sentencing, should be allowed when necessary to correct a "manifest injustice." *Frank v. Blackburn*, 646 F.2d 873 (5th Cir. 1980); *Miller v. State*, 814 So.2d 1131, 1132 (Fla. 5th DCA 2002). "Manifest injustice [occurs] whenever . . . the plea was involuntarily." *Blackburn*, 646 F.2d at 891. Thus, any time that the newly discovered evidence has a significant impact on the voluntariness of the plea, it should be alleged that withdrawal of the plea is necessary to correct the manifest injustice.

Trial courts are often skeptical of newly discovered evidence claims, especially relating to recanted testimony. Nevertheless, if a valid newly discovered evidence is available, Rule 3.850 provides a vehicle for presenting a postconviction attack based on the newly discovered evidence. It is important to be aware of the required elements of newly discovered evidence claim (for either a conviction after trial or a plea) and to properly allege each element listed above. Speculative or conclusory allegations will not carry such a claim. But, if there is a legitimate newly discovered evidence issue, this may be a valid way to either withdraw a plea or obtain a new trial.

LIMITING USE of EVIDENTIARY HEARING TESTIMONY

It has long been a concern of mine that testimony given during a postconviction evidentiary hearing will be used against my client at a retrial. This is because when a 3.850 motion involves questions of attorney ineffectiveness, the movant must waive his attorney-client privilege relating to conversations with the original trial/plea attorney. *See, Lopez v. Singletery*, 634 So.2d 1054 (Fla. 1993). Likewise, if the postconviction movant has to testify to support any claims, there is the possibility that the prosecutor could attempt to exploit the situation to elicit admissions about the case from the defendant, which could then later be used against the defendant at a retrial (if one is granted). Unfortunately, there is no Florida caselaw that adequately addresses this situation. As a result, I have made it my pet issue to get the Florida Courts to address such a situation.

In any postconviction case where an evidentiary hearing is granted, the above concerns will likely arise. Therefore, I advise filing a motion, prior to the evidentiary hearing, asking the court to limit the use of any privileged/protected testimony solely to the 3.850 proceedings. It should be argued that while the testimony of the trial attorney and/or the defendant are clearly relevant to the ineffectiveness of counsel claims under consideration by the court, the applicability of said evidence should be limited solely to the postconviction proceedings. In other words, it would be fundamentally unfair to allow any evidence adduced in the 3.850 proceedings to be later used against the defendant at a new trial (should one be granted). The waiver of the 3.850 movant's attorney-client privilege only occurs because of the claim of ineffectiveness of counsel. Thus, should the court grant the 3.850 motion based upon a finding of ineffectiveness of trial counsel, the defendant should not be punished as a result of his attorney's failures. Instead, the defendant should be placed in the position that he was prior to trial, i.e., that no privileged material should be presented against him.

The waiver of the attorney-client privilege and the right to remain silent should be construed narrowly so as to preclude use of confidential information at a new trial or retrial (should such a trial be granted). In *Bittaker v. Woodford*, 331 F.3d 715 (9th Cir. 2003), it was held that the scope of a habeas corpus petitioner's waiver arising from claim of ineffective assistance of counsel extended only to litigation of the federal habeas petition; and, therefore, the attorney-client privilege was not waived for all time and all purposes, including the possible retrial of the petitioner, if he was successful in setting aside his original conviction or sentence. Likewise, addressing the same issue, *U.S. v. Pinson*, 584 F.3d 972, 978 (10th Cir. 2009), held that a court must impose a waiver no broader than needed to ensure the fairness of the proceedings before it.

Also, in *Simmons v. U.S.*, 390 U.S. 377, 394, 88 S.Ct. 967, 976 (1968), it was noted that where testimony of the defendant was required to support a 4th Amendment suppression claim, an undeniable tension is created between the protection against illegal searches and seizures and the 5th Amendment protection against self-incrimination and, therefore, "when a defendant testifies in support of a motion to suppress evidence on Fourth Amendment grounds, his testimony may not thereafter be admitted against him at trial on the issue of guilt unless he makes no objection." A similar dilemma is created when a postconviction movant must testify at an evidentiary hearing; in order to support the burden of proof about ineffectiveness of a trial attorney, a defendant may have to testify and thus be subjected to questions about his case. If said testimony would later be used against the defendant at a retrial, then a tension is created between the defendant's 5th Amendment right to remain silent and his ability to adequately pursue his 6th Amendment right to effective assistance of counsel. Just as with *Simmons*, such a dilemma should be remedied by limiting the use of the postconviction movant's testimony to the collateral proceedings and precluding any use of his testimony at a retrial.

The matters addressed in this article present what appears to be a novel but important question of law in Florida. I recommend that the above arguments be raised for any 3.850 evidentiary hearing where the trial attorney and/or defendant will have to testify. It is recommended that a motion be filed in advance of the evidentiary hearing and that a ruling on the motion be requested from the court before any testimony and or evidence is presented at the 3.850 evidentiary hearing.

DID the OFFENSE
REALLY OCCUR in a DWELLING?

The question of whether a building or property is a "dwelling" can become a very relevant issue when determining the level of certain offenses. For example, a simple burglary (one where there is no assault or battery and the defendant is not armed) of a *dwelling* amounts to a second degree punishable by 15 years imprisonment. F.S. §810.02(3). On the other hand, if the act committed was actually simple burglary of an unoccupied structure or conveyance (as opposed to a dwelling), the offense is a 3rd degree felony, punishable by up to 5 years' incarceration. F.S. §810.02(4). Likewise, the nature of a building as a dwelling or structure is relevant to the charge of arson. Arson of a dwelling is a 1st degree felony, punishable by up to 30 years. F.S., §806.01(1)(a). But, arson of an unoccupied structure is a 2nd degree felony. F.S., §806.01(2). Thus, the question of whether a building is a *dwelling* or a *structure* can make a great deal of difference in the ultimate sentence in a burglary or arson case. This is an element of burglary and arson cases that is sometimes overlooked and is worth investigating for any defendants convicted of burglary or arson of a dwelling.

F.S. §810.011(2) provides that "dwelling" means "a building or conveyance of any kind, including any attached porch, whether such building or conveyance is temporary or permanent, mobile or immobile, which has a roof over it and is designed to be occupied by people lodging therein at night, together with the curtilage thereof."

Thus, there are many factors that must be analyzed to determine whether a building or property is a dwelling. One such question is whether the property at issue is a part of the curtilage (the land or yard adjoining a house). A common question is if an unattached garage is part of the curtilage of a dwelling. In *Martinez v. State*, 700 So.2d 142 (Fla. 5th DCA 1997), it was held that an unattached garage from which the defendant stole a tool was not part of the curtilage of the home. In *Martinez* the defendant was convicted of burglary of a dwelling. The burglary of a dwelling conviction arose from Martinez's theft of a tool from the garage of the victim's home. The victim testified that a driveway ran from the street to his two-car garage. The victim further said that the garage was not attached to his home and that his property was not enclosed with a fence. Martinez argued at trial that the garage was not part of the curtilage and, thus, he could not be found guilty of burglary of a dwelling. The trial court disagreed and Martinez was found guilty of burglary of a dwelling.

On appeal, the Fifth DCA noted that the Florida Supreme Court addressed the issue of what constitutes "curtilage" for the purposes of the burglary statute in *State v. Hamilton*, 660 So.2d 1038 (Fla. 1996). The *Hamilton* Court held that "some form of an enclosure [is necessary] in order for the area surrounding a residence to be considered part of the 'curtilage' as referred to in the burglary statute." The *Martinez* Court then noted that to enclose commonly means to surround on all sides. *Martinez* at 143. As such, it was held that the property in question was not "enclosed." Consequently, Martinez's conviction for burglary of a dwelling was vacated and the case was remanded for the trial court to enter a judgment of guilty of the lesser-included charge of burglary of a structure. *Id.* at 144.

Another relevant question regarding a building's dwelling status is whether the building is habitable. For the purpose of establishing that a 1st degree arson of a dwelling has been committed, the temporary absence of tenants will not cause the house to lose its character as a dwelling if the absence is not unreasonably prolonged and there is an intention to return. But, a house which is abandoned as a dwelling and closed up, or which is converted to some purpose other than human occupancy, ceases to be a dwelling. *Sawyer v. State*, 132 So. 188 (Fla. 1931); *PPM v. State*, 447 So. 2d 445 (Fla. 2nd DCA 1984); and *Mitchell v. State*, 734 So.2d 1067 (1st DCA 1999). In *Mitchell*, the 1st DCA noted that the "dwelling" in question had been vacant from 1994 through 1996 and had been cited with numerous housing violations that made the building uninhabitable. As such, the *Mitchell* Court held that a "vacant, damaged, boarded-up house is not a 'dwelling' within the meaning of section 806.01...when there is no evidence the owners intend to return." *Mitchell* at 1068.

In light of the above, it is always worthwhile to investigate whether a building is actually a dwelling for the purposes of a burglary or arson conviction. These questions are often overlooked by trial attorneys and can result in a defendant being convicted of a more serious offense than the offense that actually occurred. The question of a building's status as a dwelling can be raised on appeal if properly preserved at trial. Or, alternatively, if trial counsel failed to address the issue, it can be raised in a Rule 3.850 motion as a claim of ineffectiveness of counsel for failure to challenge the dwelling status of the building in question. (That is what happened in *Mitchell*). If said issue is raised in a 3.850 motion, both ineffectiveness of counsel and resulting prejudice must be demonstrated, as per the ineffectiveness test enunciated in *Strickland v. Washington*, 466 U.S. 668 (1984). Either way, it is always worth considering if the property in question actually qualifies as a dwelling for the purpose of the burglary and arson statutes because reduction in the severity of the offense will likely result in a significant reduction of the resulting sentence.

ABOUT the AUTHOR

Loren D. Rhoton is an attorney in private practice with the law office of Loren Rhoton, P.A., in Tampa, Florida. Mr. Rhoton graduated from the University of Toledo College of Law and has been a member in good standing with The Florida Bar since his admission to practice in 1995. The exclusive focus of Mr. Rhoton's practice is dedicated to assisting Florida inmates with their criminal appeal/postconviction cases.

Mr. Rhoton is a member of The Florida Bar's Appellate Division. He is also a member of the U.S. District Court, in and for the Middle and Northern Districts of Florida. Mr. Rhoton is licensed to practice before the U.S. Court of Appeals for the 11th Circuit and is also certified to practice before the U.S. Supreme Court. Mr. Rhoton regularly practices before Federal District Courts and the U.S. Court of Appeals for the 11th Circuit.

Mr. Rhoton typically deals with clients who have lengthy prison sentences. Mr. Rhoton has investigated and pursued hundreds of postconviction cases. He has practiced in all phases of the Florida Judicial System, all the way from misdemeanor county courts up to the Florida Supreme Court. Additionally, Mr. Rhoton has been directly responsible for amendments to Florida Rule of Criminal Procedure 3.850 (the main vehicle for most postconviction actions). Mr. Rhoton was appointed by the Florida Supreme Court to the Florida Criminal Rules Steering Committee, Subcommittee on Postconviction Relief, which focused on rewriting Florida

Rule of Criminal Procedure 3.850. Mr. Rhoton worked on said subcommittee with judges and other governmental officials in an effort to improve the administration and execution of postconviction proceedings. Mr. Rhoton's role on said committee was to advocate for changes that were beneficial to postconviction litigants.

For over a decade, Mr. Rhoton authored a bimonthly article, *Postconviction Corner*, for Florida Prison Legal Perspectives. Selected articles from *Postconviction Corner* have been compiled and printed in a legal self-help book, *Postconviction Relief for the Florida Prisoner*. Mr. Rhoton also served on the Board of Directors of the Florida Prisoners' Legal Aid Organization.

Loren Rhoton has dedicated his career to helping Florida inmates seek justice. In addition to providing criminal appeals and postconviction representation to individuals, Mr. Rhoton also volunteered his time and advice to the Florida Prison Legal Aid Organization (FPLAO). Mr. Rhoton sat on the Board of Directors of FPLAO and wrote a legal self-help column, Postconviction Corner, for FPLAO's publication, the Florida Prison Legal Perspectives. When FPLAO dissolved, Mr. Rhoton continued to offer his self-help articles in his own newsletter, the Florida Postconviction Journal. This book is a compilation of Mr. Rhoton's articles from FPLP and the Florida Postconviction Journal.

Contact Loren Rhoton at:
412 E. Madison Street
Suite 1111
Tampa, Florida 33602
Email: *lorenrhoton@rhotonpostconviction.com*
Website: www.rhotonpostconviction.com

www.ingramcontent.com/pod-product-compliance
Lightning Source LLC
Chambersburg PA
CBHW071505200326
41519CB00019B/5878